Contents

Preface

The key role that external influences play in the way businesses operate and the decisions they make has been recognized in the prominent coverage given to them in the AS and A level specifications. This new book explains those external factors in a very lucid and informed way.

It should prove to be particularly useful for students studying for:

- AQA's AS level Module 3 and A level Module 6
- Edexcel's AS level Unit 1 and A level Unit 6
- OCR's AS level Module 2871 and A level Module 2878.

The author, Nancy Wall, is well known and respected for her role as co-founder and co-ordinator of the Nuffield Economics and Business Project. She is also a research fellow of the University of Sussex and has a wealth of experience as a teacher, trainer and writer.

Susan Grant
Series Editor

Introduction

All businesses have to face changes in the circumstances under which they operate. These are the *external influences* which, by definition, the business can do nothing to control. Changing circumstances may create favourable opportunities or problems.

Chapter 1 looks at the way in which market forces affect the business situation. A good understanding of how the forces of supply and demand work in the relevant market can help managers to avoid losses.

The level of competition in the market has crucial effects on individual businesses. *Chapter 2* covers different market situations that can arise.

Chapter 3 looks at the nature of the whole economy. It focuses on economic growth, the business cycle, the impact of international trade and the effects of exchange rate changes.

The subject of *Chapter 4* is government economic policy. Particular attention is given to tax and interest rate policies, as well as exchange rate policy and EMU. The controversial nature of these policy decisions is highlighted.

Technology affects businesses in very different ways. *Chapter 5* investigates the roles of product and process innovation, considers the impact of new technologies on society, and looks at how new ways and new products may affect individuals.

Social and cultural influences, dealt with in *Chapter 6*, have very diverse elements. Population changes and cultural preferences affect consumer product choices. Rising standards apply both to products and to the way businesses relate to their employees. Education affects consumer choices and changes the options open to employees.

Chapter 7 concentrates on legal influences, looking in detail at consumer protection, competition law, and many aspects of employment law.

There is a fine line between legal and political influences. The latter is the subject matter of *Chapter 8* and concerns the level of government intervention and its development over the years in the UK and in Europe.

Chapter 9 takes in the environment: the ecological environment as opposed to the business environment. Here we are concerned with the idea of sustainable development, external costs and public environmental anxieties.

Ethical business, the subject matter of *Chapter 10*, develops themes already introduced in order to address issues relating to business responsibility.

Chapter One

Markets

'May you live in interesting times' Ancient Chinese proverb

External influences on businesses are many and varied; by their nature, they are changing all the time. So all business decisions must be taken against the background of the external factors which are important for the business in question. The success of the decisions will depend on how accurately the decision-takers have assessed the external influences. By definition, these are influences which they cannot control.

Perhaps the biggest influences on many businesses come from the **markets** in which they operate. The level of sales they can realistically achieve may be greatly affected by **market forces**. These forces impact on the business from two angles:

- the number of other businesses in the market – the **competition**

- the level of customer **demand.**

An example will show how these two aspects of market forces interact. The boxed case study 'Cruise away' is based on several newspaper reports which appeared early in 2001.

Case study: Cruise away

Cruise liner companies are cutting their prices again. Several of them have taken delivery of new liners, increasing capacity in the business. They're competing aggressively and hoping to attract more people than ever before.

They may not succeed. The slowdown in the American economy seems likely to discourage at least a few potential customers. Incomes are growing slowly there now, and your planned ocean cruise is one of the first things you might cut back on. The UK market for luxury holidays still looks fairly buoyant, but even there, job losses in manufacturing could threaten the cruise companies.

Price cutting may or may not help the individual company to maintain its market share. If they all cut prices by similar amounts, they may all end up with lower profits. On the other hand, they may be able to attract new customers who were put off by the old, higher prices. Margins will be lower, but this may not matter too much if occupancy rates are high.

Market forces and business decisions

Two crucial things happened to cruise operators in the 1990s.

- Incomes were growing strongly in much of Europe and North America. Demand for luxury products grew quite fast.

- Decisions were taken to build and operate more cruise liners.

It made sense for the businesses which organized the cruises to invest in increased capacity. Cruises were proving very profitable.

Unfortunately, just as the new liners came on stream, in 2000, the US economy was slowing down. Demand generally began to grow much more slowly than it had for some years. The cruise operators increased capacity too much, just at a time when passenger growth was slowing down. The companies responded by cutting prices in an attempt to fill the extra cabins.

Did the individual companies which bought new liners each know that they were not alone? Should they have been able to predict the slowdown in the American economy? Would they have reacted differently if they had known about these trends? We cannot know the answers to these questions, but we can see that paying attention to the business environment before taking decisions can be very important. A gap between the supply of cruise holidays and the customers' demand for them could seriously dent the profits of the companies in the business.

Opportunities and constraints

Growing markets create opportunities. There will be enough demand for the product for all producers to expand. The competition may not be much of a constraint because all the businesses experience rising sales. Growing markets may come from rising incomes, but they may also come from changes in the pattern of demand. A new product may attract a lot of customers – think of micro-scooters. A change in fashions can leave one product out in the cold and create a bonanza for another.

Shrinking or even static markets produce a different story. Competing businesses will struggle to hold on to existing customers. They may compete on price; they may also compete on quality and design. Non-price competition of all kinds becomes vitally important. There may be aggressive advertising campaigns and all kinds of promotions. Some businesses will find cost savings which will fund price cuts. Or they may diversify, cutting production of the slow-moving item and developing new products.

Analysing market forces

Supply and demand analysis can help to clarify what is happening when market forces are active. In Figure 1, the demand curve slopes downwards – indicating the usual relationship between price and quantity sold. Cutting the price will normally lead to more of the product being produced and sold. The supply curve is sloping upwards – so the higher the price, the greater the incentive to produce and the more output will rise.

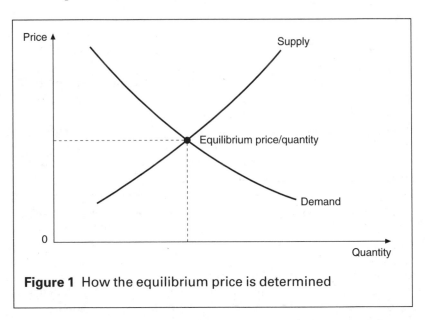

Figure 1 How the equilibrium price is determined

The supply and demand curves intersect at the equilibrium price. This is important because it shows that there is a price and a level of output at which producers can sell all they produce and consumers get all they want to buy.

Thinking again about micro-scooters, and using supply and demand analysis, we can show that as the product caught on, the demand curve was shifting to the right. Figure 2 shows that at a whole range of possible prices, consumers want more micro-scooters. We can predict that as demand rises, the price will rise. Output rises too – it is profitable to increase the quantity supplied. Businesses are responding to the increased demand and rising profits. Resources are being moved into micro-scooter production.

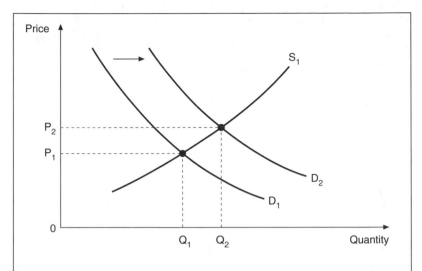

Figure 2 The effect of a shift of the demand curve to the right

Applying the theory

Now see whether you can use the same kind of analysis for the cruise liners. This situation is not the exact mirror image of the micro-scooter example. Here we have a static market: it appears that demand for cruises simply stopped growing – so the demand curve stayed exactly the same. What did change was the number of cabins available – the supply. It's useful in this situation to think of the supply as being a vertical line – the level of output, or the number of cabins available. This moved: it shifted to the right because the companies bought more liners. Sketch the diagram for yourself.

What is the prediction? Cruise prices will fall as companies compete to get the available customers. But what happens if this situation

---

Entry and exit

When attractive profits are being made, it is likely that firms will enter the industry. They will respond to growing demand by moving resources into profitable lines of production. The reverse happens when demand is falling. Profits will fall and losses may be made. Some businesses will decide on exit as the best strategy. Sometimes this process is called the 'profit-signalling mechanism', because it usually ensures that businesses respond to changes in consumer demand.

persists? It's quite likely that some of the companies will find cruises less profitable than they had hoped. Some may not be able to cover the costs of running the new liners. Eventually they will sell up if profits seem unlikely to improve. This is called exit from the market.

Changing demand

When demand is increasing, two things happen.

- Some new businesses move into the market.

- Existing producers expand.

Some resources – capital equipment and people – stop producing the things for which demand is falling. They move off into products for which demand is growing. (Of course, in practice, they are often not the same resources.) The incentive of profit makes it worthwhile to change. The flow chart in Figure 3 shows how the process works.

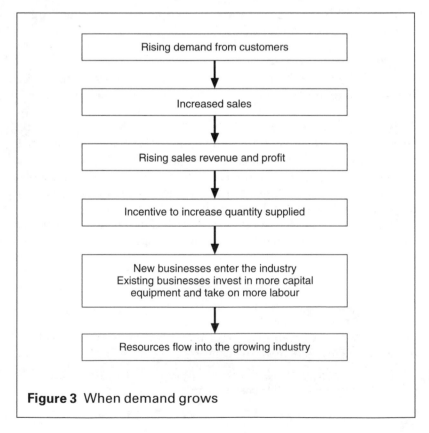

Figure 3 When demand grows

The pattern of consumer demand is constantly changing, so profits will be developing in different products all the time. This is why market forces create a dynamic system. Businesses strive to keep up with the changes. If they cannot keep up, they become progressively less profitable and eventually close down. You can reverse the flow chart to trace the process of exit from the market.

It is worth remembering that markets do not always work quite like this. Some businesses develop enormous power in their markets and look for ways to influence potential customers. Some governments want to influence markets for a variety of reasons. Sometimes governments provide certain products because they are considered essential and not everyone would be able to afford them. (Did you yourself pay for this book?) In these circumstances market forces work in different ways.

Later chapters will take up a range of issues which spring from the ways in which markets actually work.

What makes demand change?

The important factors which influence demand are:

- incomes

- tastes and fashions

- the prices of competing substitutes.

So far, in the cruise example, we have seen that incomes can be an important influence on demand. How important that influence is depends on the product. You can probably work out straight away how you would spend an increase in income. Your spending on toothpaste and soap probably wouldn't change at all.

Tastes and fashions can be very important for some products. Demand for red meat has been falling slowly for some years, as people heard more and more about the effects of particular meat products on health. Demand for chicken has grown.

Competing substitutes often turn out to have a vital impact on the individual business. Often particular brands are very good substitutes – as with baked beans. But new technologies can spell trouble for whole industries. Synthetic fibres have had a long-lasting impact on demand for woollens. Some competing substitutes come from producers abroad with lower costs. Look underneath your telephone – it has almost certainly come from China.

Changes in supply

Markets are greatly affected by new technologies. These affect the range of products available and costs of production. Process innovation refers to the way in which production methods can be improved by using new technologies. This will mean lower costs of production.

Over the years a wide range of manufactured products have become cheaper to produce. Businesses in the relevant industries which cannot cut costs in this way find it hard to compete. They usually have to stop producing eventually. Chapter 5 looks at the impact of new technologies in more detail.

When costs are falling in this way, the effects can be shown as in Figure 4. The supply curve shifts downwards. Producers may benefit from higher profits for a while, especially if they have developed a new process themselves. In time, competition will normally force prices down so that customers benefit. Then it may be possible to sell a larger quantity (think of TVs or computers).

Change and the business

Thinking about market forces, it is easy to see why some businesses are risky. Coping with the kind of changes discussed so far is never easy.

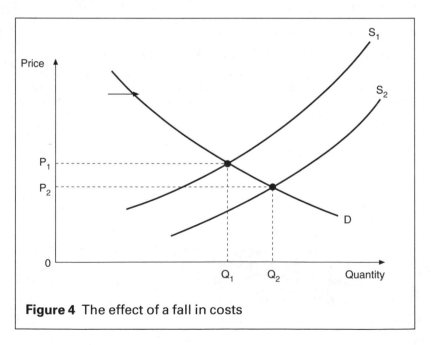

Figure 4 The effect of a fall in costs

But big swings in market conditions are quite common. Some kinds of businesses are much more vulnerable than others, but all businesses need to be able to adapt and to be good at problem-solving.

One way for a business to protect itself is to have good market research procedures. These will give warning of changes in market demand. Sometimes the changes will be qualitative rather than quantitative. In clothing production, people will not usually stop buying clothes but they may well turn against particular styles. Big businesses will try to lead the market if they can but smaller producers may have to be followers.

Excess capacity

It often happens that market changes leave some businesses with excess capacity. The cruise liner owners were in this position. The steel industry has suffered from excess capacity for many years now. It is becoming a problem in the car industry too. In both cases, world capacity is perhaps 20 per cent above current world demand. Some of this excess capacity was in the UK, at the Corus steel-making plants. Excess capacity was also an important reason for the closure of the Vauxhall car plant at Luton in early 2001.

Excess capacity can be caused by falling demand. In the case of steel, other materials have been developed and competition has reduced the

---

Case study: Corus closes Llanwern

Corus was formed in 1999 from British Steel and Hoogovens of the Netherlands. Very soon, the management had to face the problems. In the year 2000, 4500 employees were made redundant from the UK workforce. Still this was not enough.

Over the period from 1970 to 1999, steel consumption in the UK fell by 49 per cent. (It fell in Germany and the US too.) Partly, this reflected a big decline in steel-using industries in the UK. Demand for UK products has shifted towards the service sector. Then, too, some industrial products and processes now use materials other than steel, often new kinds of plastics (think of car bumpers). The high value of the pound after 1997 made UK steel less competitive in EU markets. Falling steel prices on world markets created yet more trouble.

During 2000, the losses from the UK steel plants amounted to £350 million. Other parts of the business made a profit. The decision to close down the iron and steel plant at Llanwern, near Newport, and the tin-plating factory at Ebbw Vale, both in South Wales, was inevitable. The workforce was described at the time as 'heroically productive'. Corus put most of the blame on the high pound.

---

size of the market. But cars – can demand be falling? It is not. However, demand for different types of vehicle is changing. In any case, the car manufacturers have created too much capacity. Some older plants have failed to modernize sufficiently and find it hard to compete with the newer plants. So some closures are inevitable.

Summarizing, there are times when the best decision is to close some or all of the business.

Capacity constraints

After pondering sad stories of decline and closures, you might think that growing demand and increasing output would be problem-free. The problems are indeed smaller but they still exist.

Sometimes demand grows so fast that it is impossible for the business to increase its capacity at the speed needed to keep up. This may lead to delay in fulfilling orders. Some trade may be lost as a result. The business may be in a strong enough position to raise prices, but this is not always its best long-run strategy if it wants to build customer loyalty.

What kinds of problems lead to the business having insufficient capacity? Any of its inputs may be in short supply:

- Space may be inadequate. Planning regulations may make it difficult to enlarge the premises quickly.

- More equipment may be needed. Suppliers of equipment may have capacity constraints too. Deliveries may be delayed, perhaps by up to a year or more.

- There may not be enough suitably skilled people available in the travel-to-work area. Training takes time and is sometimes costly.

- Even shortages of raw materials or key components may cause delays and cost increases.

The Confederation of British Industry (CBI) collects data on the number of businesses reporting that shortages of skilled labour may constrain output. The data is shown in Table 1.

The impact of international markets

International trade has been growing fast for some time. Take a look at Figure 5, which shows the data for world output and world trade growth.

Table 1 Percentage of businesses expecting lack of skilled labour to constrain output in the next four months

Month	Percentage
October 1997	17
April 1998	15
October 1998	8
April 1999	6
October 1999	11
April 2000	14
October 2000	17
April 2001	17

Source: *National Institute Economic Review*, 2001.

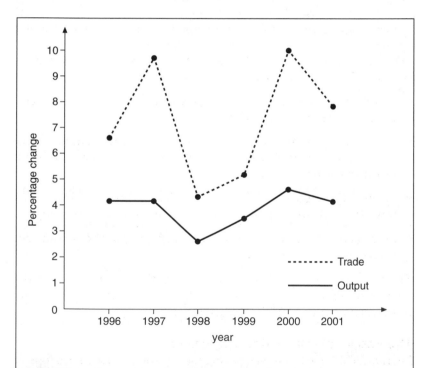

Figure 5 Percentage changes in world output and world trade (IMF figures)

Growing trade means that businesses are getting access to larger markets. This may enable them to expand – or it may simply allow them to survive in the face of competition in their domestic markets.

Sometimes a business which has been exporting successfully will actually set up production facilities in the country to which it has been exporting. This will turn it into a multinational company, sometimes also called a transnational. Some very big companies like Unilever and Coca Cola have operations in most of the world's countries, and their brands are recognized internationally.

This means that many of the external influences on business actually come from international trends. In Chapter 3 the implications of this will be explored further.

KEY WORDS

External influences	Supply
Markets	Equilibrium price
Market forces	Entry
Competition	Exit
Demand	Process innovation
Profits	Excess capacity
Capacity	Capacity constraints

Further reading

Bamford, C., and Munday, S., Chapters 1–4 in *Markets*, Heinemann Educational, 2002.

Barnes, S., Chapter 1 in *Essential Business*, 2nd edn, Collins, 1997.

Chambers, I., and Gray, D., Chapter 17 in *Business Studies*, 2nd edn, Causeway, 2000.

'Consumer markets', in the *Marketing Pocket Book*, NTC Publications, 2001.

Marcouse, I. (ed.), Unit 60 in *Business Studies*, or Unit 41 in *Business Studies for AS*, Hodder & Stoughton, 1999 and 2001 respectively.

Useful websites

For data on meat consumption, go to www.bized.ac.uk and look for Company Facts and the Meat and Livestock Commission. Select the question 'What is the consumption of meat products?'

Essay topic
Using a business you have studied, describe the market in which it operates. Explain the impact on the business of recent changes in the market.

Data response question
The following is taken from *Metro*, 3 May 2001. Read the piece and then answer the questions.

Whitbread creates 4000 new jobs

Hotels and leisure group Whitbread is to create more than 4000 jobs in the next three years. The company, which last month sold its pubs and bars division for £1.63 billion, announced a £200 million expansion.

It plans to open a further 80 Brewers Fayre and Brewsters pub-restaurants by the end of 2004. Ten new David Lloyd Leisure clubs will open by the end of next year.

More than 3000 full- and part-time staff will be recruited by Brewers Fayre, while 1000 employees will staff the new health clubs. Recruitment could be almost doubled by plans to open another 100 Travel Inns in the near future.

News of the expansion came as the company said it had made a 'flying start' to life as a smaller business. Although pre-tax profits fell 4 per cent to £335 million in the year to 3 March, Whitbread Hotels' managing director Alan Parker said its remaining businesses, which include Marriott Hotels, Pizza Hut and Costa Coffee, had shown strong growth.

He added that the Leeds region would see £12 million of investment and 140 new jobs, while there would be £26 million invested in the Manchester area, creating 500 jobs.

1. What features do the component parts of the Whitbread group have in common? [4 marks]
2. Explain why Whitbread might expect to be able to expand so rapidly. [8 marks]
3. What problems do you think the business might encounter as it expands? [8 marks]

Chapter Two

Competition

'A firm can be defined as a set of contracts and relationships. Added value is created by its success in putting these contracts and relationships together, so it is the quality and distinctiveness of these contracts that promote added value.'
John Kay, in *The Business of Economics* (1996)

Competition everywhere?

Just now and then, a business is able to carve out a market which it can keep for itself alone. A shop selling organic, additive-free meat and other organic foods in a small town might manage to capture most of the local market if the competing supermarkets are not trying very hard in this area. Other people who might consider setting up a similar business may reckon that the market is not big enough for two shops to be profitable. But this situation is sure to be unusual. Even Microsoft, which must be about the most powerful business in the world, has some competition.

The nature of the competition, though, will vary greatly. Any time we are looking at the market for a particular product, we need to ask some searching questions about it in order to understand the competitive situation.

- Are there many businesses in the same market?

- Are they all selling products which are very similar, or do the products compete partly on their individual features?

- Is it important to be able to develop new and improved products in this market?

- Is it possible for new businesses to get started?

- Is there a price leader in this market, a business which is strong enough to set prices, which others will be obliged to follow?

Answering these questions will help us to decide how strong the competition is for an individual business. If there are many sellers, all selling broadly similar products and it is easy for new businesses to come into the market, then competition will be stiff. This might apply to producers of fruit and vegetables. Price is going to be important: growers who cannot keep costs and prices down at levels similar to those of their competitors are unlikely to survive for long.

Yet competition can be quite stiff in markets which are not at all like that for fruit and vegetables. Take, for example, car markets. There are relatively few producers, they make very varied models, and technical improvements are introduced all the time. Yet they must compete – on price, or quality, style or reliability.

Market categories
We give rather precise definitions to particular market categories. In practice, markets don't always fit neatly into these categories, but they can still help us to distinguish their different characteristics (see Table 2).

Monopoly
Monopolies are unusual. BT used to have a monopoly as a telephone provider in the UK, when it was a nationalized industry. Since then, the price of a phone call has come down because of improved technologies, but also because of competition in the industry. Some railway lines still have an effective monopoly, although many compete with road travel

Table 2 Market categories

Category	Features
Perfect competition	Many sellers
	Easy entry to the market
	Identical products irrespective of the producer
	All use the same technologies
	Market information is easy to obtain
	Price is set by the market
Monopolistic competition	Many sellers
	Easy entry
	Differentiated products
Oligopoly	Small number of dominant sellers
	Barriers to entry
	Differentiated products
	Some businesses are price makers
	Sellers are interdependent
Monopoly	A single seller
	Barriers to entry
	Price can be controlled

and some with the airlines. Microsoft are quite close to having a monopoly because they can exploit our need for compatibility with their patented products and their links to the hardware suppliers. Monopolies cannot survive without **barriers to entry**. These can be legal, as in the story of BT, or wherever patents are important in protecting new inventions. Or the barriers can be to do with the high cost of entry and the advantages which big producers enjoy. Building a second railway line or paying for the advertising needed to compete effectively with Microsoft are not practical options for a new business.

Oligopoly

Oligopolies, in contrast, are quite common. Cars have already been mentioned. Here again, barriers to entry are important. These may come from high initial costs (like development, design and capital investment in machinery, as with cars). They may also come from heavy advertizing costs, as with cleaning products. Two firms, Unilever and Proctor & Gamble, dominate the market for washing products and advertize very extensively. A newcomer to this market has to have a large advertizing budget in order to compete at all.

Wherever large-scale production costs less than small-scale production (that is there are economies of scale), there will be tendency for oligopolies to develop.

Despite the barriers to entry, oligopolies typically exhibit fierce competition. The businesses involved watch one another's strategies and their advertising and pricing policies. They design their reactions accordingly.

Monopolistic competition

With monopolistic competition, there is easy entry and this makes a big difference. Restaurants invariably present a picture of monopolistic competition. They compete on their individual, sometimes unique, qualities. Entry is easy – newcomers set up in business all the time. In order to compete, they have to be perceived as offering value for money. So only the ones with the highest reputations for cooking and serving the food can charge the fanciest prices. Competition is often very stiff.

Perfect competition

Perfect competition does not apply only to fruit and vegetables. Although there are almost always ways in which competition is not quite perfect, you can see something very similar in any commodity market, where the output of one producer is indistinguishable from the next – iron ore, wheat, sugar and many raw materials are like this. Having said that, the world banana market is dominated by two companies, Geests and Elders & Fyffes, even though it is impossible to distinguish their products from one another.

Some manufacturers are quite like perfect competitors too. If you are producing components for cars, you will be competing with many other suppliers, all of whom face the same quality requirements set by the car manufacturers. To get the orders, you will have to keep the price to a minimum.

Competitive advantage

In order to survive, almost all businesses need to find sources of **competitive advantage**. We can divide these into groups:

- Cost advantages, which can give the business cost leadership, might come from efficient human resource management, or stock control mechanisms, or innovative production methods or good supplier relationships. Cost advantages can be very important in helping the business to compete on price.

- Product advantages arise as extra value is added to products in a variety of ways. These include innovations of all kinds, both new product development and improvements in design and reliability; image enhancements, either real or through advertising and branding; and all the other ways in which businesses seek to add value and improve their reputations.

Notice how the sources of competitive advantage can be linked to various elements in the 4 Ps.

Competing on price

Only a few businesses can set price without serious consideration of the competition. Even a luxury country house hotel charging very high prices will have to provide many attractive features in order to be perceived as offering value for money.

Sometimes, businesses operating in an oligopoly situation get involved in a **price war**. These have been seen among the petrol companies, in the travel business, among newspapers, channel ferries and airlines. Price wars do not usually last for very long, because the participants will always face a fall in profits. Sometimes the motive for starting a price war is the belief that the weakest competitor will be forced out of business. *The Times* hoped to get rid of *The Independent* in this way. The idea is that after the price war has done its job, the

Ryanair steps up price war with rival Go

Ryanair, Europe's leading low-cost airline, is intensifying its price war with Go, the rival no-frills carrier, on routes between Scotland and Dublin.

Go, which was sold in June by British Airways to a management buy-out, provoked Ryanair into starting the first price war between rival low-cost airlines in Europe, announcing the launch of services from Edinburgh and Glasgow to Dublin, Ryanair's home base.

Ryanair pre-empted the Go move by starting its own Dublin to Edinburgh flights last week, adding to a flood of extra capacity on routes between Scotland and Ireland. As promotional launch fares plunged, Ryanair eventually cut prices to £10 return for every seat on the Dublin services to Edinburgh and Glasgow for two months. Ryanair is now further increasing pressure on Go, whose finances are weaker.

With five daily return flights between Dublin and Edinburgh, Ryanair claims the route has become its most successful launch with only 341 of 60,000 seats left unsold, albeit at give-away prices. Aer Lingus, the Irish state-owned carrier, is expected to be the main casualty of the fight between Ryanair and Go.

Financial Times, 3 September 2001

remaining players in the market will pick up the extra customers and return to charging higher prices. This can enhance profitability considerably. With one competitor departing, market share can increase for the rest.

Competing on price does not necessarily involve price wars. Simply by offering the product at the best price they can achieve, businesses can expand their markets. When prices fall because technologies are changing, it is possible for all producers to benefit from the increased sales of the industry as a whole.

This has happened with air travel. Over the long run, better aircraft design and lower running costs have brought air travel down to prices which many more people can afford. At the same time, on the demand side, rising incomes had been enlarging the market prior to 11 September 2001. New entrants like Virgin and easyJet had been able to come into the market. Competition had increased but there had been room in the market for many airlines to expand. All fight hard to increase their market share.

In the short run or when the total market size is more or less stable, competition can drive out the less-efficient, higher-cost businesses. The airlines will be interesting to watch: if demand picks up again and they expand too much, excess capacity could have a disastrous effect on profits and lead quickly to serious problems.

When competition increases

More competition means more competing products in the marketplace. If they compete, it follows that they are substitutes for one another. People can switch from one to another, shop around looking for the best price. A price cut will usually lead to a rise in the quantity demanded.

Price elasticity of demand

Price elasticity of demand measures the responsiveness of quantity demanded to a change in price. The formula is:

$$\text{Price elasticity of demand} = \frac{\text{per cent change in quantity demanded}}{\text{per cent change in price}}$$

Normally, price elasticity is negative because a rise in price leads to a fall in quantity demanded. If the number itself is greater than one, then demand responds more than proportionately to a change in price and demand is said to be elastic. A price cut will bring increased sales and rising turnover.

Businesses can use their past sales records and their market research to estimate the price elasticity of demand for their products. They can work out what the effect of a price increase is likely to be in terms of lost sales, or vice versa.

When there is easy entry and other businesses are coming into the market with competing products, a rise in price is more than likely to lead to a fall in demand for the product. There will be more competing products and they may be good substitutes for one another. Increasing competition means that price elasticity of demand will rise. The business will have to be careful to keep its prices down. Both price and non-price competition may become increasingly important.

Non-price competition

Deciding how best to compete is a process that will vary considerably from one product to another. But with many products, whether customers perceive it as offering value for money depends on the features of the product itself. For example, ready-cooked meals have to have appetising flavours as well as convenience in use. The product will have to be carefully developed and tested to ensure that people actually enjoy it. Similarly all mechanical products will be expected to be reliable and will lose their reputation if they are not.

Other products depend for their markets on the effectiveness of their advertising. Toys provide numerous examples. It is hard for a new toy to carve out a market for itself without advertising. The toy producers battle for market share on the television screens every Saturday morning. Price competition seems to be largely irrelevant. Having an initially attractive product clearly helps but the main thrust of the competitive effort is to be seen in the adverts. Market share becomes an important measure of success.

First-mover advantage

Businesses which succeed in competitive industries usually have a history of innovation. As soon as their competitors start to copy their ideas, they are ready to move on. This means that they need a corporate culture which is favourable to continuous innovation. Corning provides an interesting example of continuing technical developments from the US.

Corning

In 1908, Corning was one of the first US companies to set up a research laboratory. By 1912, it introduced a new glass baking dish made of Pyrex. The company had discovered a type of glass which conducted heat better than metal. The firm's objective was to use scientific breakthroughs to meet the needs of the market.

From this initial advantage Corning went on to develop specialist glass products for use in medicine, telecommunications, consumer electronics and missiles. There are relatively few firms competing in the speciality glass industry. This gives Corning an advantage – its technical mastery creates barriers for potential new entrants. But specialists tend to find that they depend on a few big customers. Corning specialized for a while in making television tubes. When the US TV manufacturers succumbed to competition from imports, Corning lost their market too.

Despite problems from time to time, the tradition of innovation has served the company well over the long term. Parts for military rockets and ceramic capsules for catalytic converters have succeeded. Now, demand is down for fibre-optic glass because of the dire position of the telecommunications industry, but work is continuing on diesel filters which could be a winner in the future.

Another example comes from the way businesses have in recent years used IT in innovative ways to develop a competitive advantage.

Fair or unfair?

Genuine product improvements and efforts to cut costs by managing the business more effectively would always be regarded as fair competition. But quite often, competing businesses will go to lengths which seem very unfair. Exactly what is unfair can be very much a matter of opinion.

Many businesses compete by locating their production processes in places where wages are low. This enables them to charge lower prices. The consumer's income can be made to go further. Quite often the people getting the low wages are better off too, especially if they did not previously have jobs. This is part of the process of globalization, which can improve standards of living.

On the other hand, some argue that using cheap labour to make all or part of the product is **unfair competition**. They believe it is wrong to pay low wages. Relocating production can lead to job losses. This view raises very difficult issues about what the wage rate for the job should be. Some people think the wage rate should be the lowest amount the business must pay to get someone to do the work. Others believe that the wage should guarantee some minimum standard of living.

Unfair competition due to low wages is part of a political debate. In contrast, there are some kinds of unfair competition which are actually recognized as such by the law. Where this is the case, businesses can make complaints to the Office of Fair Trading, which implements the government's competition policies. (Competition law will be dealt with

---

easyJet and Go

The no-frills airlines compete fiercely. Early in 2001, easyJet complained to the Advertizing Standards Authority (ASA) that its rival, Go, was misleading passengers as to the real cost of flights.

Go claimed that its fares to Nice for the Monaco Grand Prix race were 40 per cent lower than easyJet's. This was only true if you compared the two airlines' highest prices. Go had also failed to make it clear that passengers would have to stay five or more nights to get the lowest fares.

Go had decided to use aggressive advertizing in its battle with easyJet. At one point, Go said that it had launched its Nice service in order to provide Stelios Haji-Ioannou, the founder of easyJet, with a better choice of flights to his tax haven home in Monaco.

The ASA upheld easyJet's complaint about misleading advertizing.

---

in more depth in Chapter 7). If the unfair competition involves advertizing, then the complaint is more likely to go to the Advertizing Standards Authority.

The benefits of competition

Michael Porter, the distinguished professor at Harvard Business School, has researched the impact of competition in great detail. He has shown that competition can help to create world-class businesses with strong competitive advantages. Strong competition in the domestic market gives businesses a big incentive to innovate and become expert with new technologies. The spur of domestic competition, causing businesses to strive for excellence in all their operations, can eventually give them an enormous advantage in international markets. By contrast, not having to compete usually makes firms flabby rather than dynamic.

In his important 1990 book, *The Competitive Advantage of Nations* (Macmillan), Porter identified a number of industries where clusters of very competitive businesses had developed. These include printing presses in Germany, patient monitoring systems in the US, ceramic tiles in Italy and robotics in Japan.

In the same book (p. 171), Porter also spelt out what *not* to do.

'Lack of pressure and challenge means that firms fail to look constantly for and interpret new buyer needs, new technologies, and new processes. They lose the stomach to make old competitive advantages obsolete in the process of creating new ones. They hesitate to employ global strategies to offset local factor disadvantages, or to tap selectively into advantages available in other nations. They are deterred by arrogance, lack of rivalry, and an unwillingness to upset the status quo and sacrifice current profits.'

Competition is good for you!

KEY WORDS

Perfect competition	Innovation
Monopolistic competition	Competing on price
Oligopoly	Price war
Monopoly	Price elasticity of demand
Barriers to entry	Non-price competition
Competitive advantage	First-mover advantage

Further reading

Campbell, D., Stonehouse, G., and Houston, B., Chapter 7 in *Business Strategy*, Butterworth–Heinemann, 1999.

Gillespie, A., Chapter 2 in *Competitive Environment and External Influences*, Hodder & Stoughton, 2000.

Griffiths, R., and Ison, S., Chapters 3–6 in *Business Economics*, Heinemann Educational, 2001.

Kay, J., Chapter 7 in *The Business of Economics*, Oxford University Press, 1996

Scholes, K., and Wales, J., 'In search of a strategy' in *Teaching Business and Economics*, The Journal of the Economics and Business Education Association 2000 (provides detail on how businesses frame their response to the pressures of competition).

Useful websites

Much useful information can be obtained from company websites. You can learn something about competition by comparing the big supermarket chains' sites. Never mind the URL, use Google for your search engine and put in the name of the business: www.google.com.

Essay topic

Why do some industries have many small competing businesses, while others have a few big firms, often with a clear market leader with power to influence the price throughout the industry? In your answer, use as many examples as you can.

Data response question

Study the following two tables from *The Marketing Pocket Book 2002*. They give information on the structure of the retail grocery trade in Great Britain. Then answer the questions.

Table A Estimated shop numbers and turnover shares by type of organization

	Number of shops		Shares of turnover (%)	
	1971	*2000*	*1971*	*2000*
Co-operatives	7745	2279	13.2	6.8
Multiples	10973	6875	44.3	87.8
Independents	86565	24487	42.5	5.5

Table B Sales of multiple grocers in (£ million) year to end Jan 2000

	Sales
Tesco	16133
Sainsbury	10840
ASDA	9198
Safeway	7121
Somerfield	3389
Kwik Save	2447
Wm. Morrison	2775
Waitrose	1898
Iceland	1859
Co-ops (combined)	1742
Savacentre	923
Aldi	782
Budgens	497
Netto	377

1. What important changes have taken place in grocery sales since 1971? [3 marks]
2. Describe the market structure of the grocery business, making reference to the data and explaining your answer. [3 marks]
3. In what ways do supermarkets compete? [3 marks]
4. In what ways might the supermarkets' efforts to compete benefit their customers? [3 marks]
5. Some supermarket suppliers claim that supermarkets use their market power to beat down food prices. How is it that they are able to do this? [3 marks]
6. Devise a strategy for a supermarket that wishes to increase its market share. [5 marks]

Chapter Three

The economy

'There are many economic puzzles, but there are only two great mysteries. One of these mysteries is why economic growth takes place at different rates over time and across countries. The other mystery is the reason why there is a business cycle.'
Paul Krugman, in *Peddling Prosperity* (1994)

Local, national and international

Around all of us there is a local economy. There are resources, production opportunities and output. There are decision-makers – consumers, producers and government agencies of many kinds. Each of these is located in a complex set of relationships which enables people to provide for their needs.

Some of these relationships are local. You, your nearest supermarket and your place of work will all be a part of the local economy. But this will be much influenced by the regional and the national economy. Many decisions are national in scope.

Increasingly, businesses and governments take their decisions within an international framework. Businesses look for international markets. Governments need to collaborate and negotiate with other governments and international organizations in order to protect the interests of their populations.

Change and opportunity

Economies change constantly, in three particular ways.

First, resources are constantly moving from one use to another. People make decisions to consume products which they did not previously buy, and vice versa. Realizing you can afford a mobile phone, deciding not to go out tonight, buying a book – all these look like small decisions, but taken across the whole economy, they spell change. Mobile phone sales grew spectacularly, but eventually most people who can afford one will have one, and then there will just be replacement sales. Pubs have been closing because people are visiting them less often. Bookshops have flourished, becoming both bigger and more numerous.

This reallocation of resources is called **structural change**. It creates both threats and opportunities for businesses, depending on whether

Table 3 Households' final consumption expenditure in the UK in 1999 (percentage of total)

	1991	1999
Goods		
Cars and other vehicles	4.5	5.1
Other durable goods	3.9	5.9
Food and household	11.6	10.4
Alcohol and tobacco	9.9	7.3
Clothing and footwear	5.5	6.9
Energy products	6.9	5.4
Other goods	11.7	13.6
Total goods	53.8	54.4
Services		
Rental and water charges	13.9	12.4
Catering	9.0	8.6
Transport and communication	8.6	9.9
Financial services	4.0	4.2
Other services	11.0	10.4
Total services	46.5	45.6

Source: ONS, *Annual Abstract of Statistics*, 2001

they face declining or growing demand. Table 3 shows changes in the pattern of consumer demand in the UK.

Second, more often than not, most economies have achieved some economic growth. Historically, the increase in world output since 1945 has been spectacular. But so far, the growth process has been erratic for most countries, most of the time. Businesses are often able to tap into growing markets because rising incomes create increased demand. But they also have serious bad patches when demand shrinks because everyone is spending less. An important element in business decision-making involves knowing how to exploit the opportunities when demand is growing and survive periods of falling demand. Figure 6 shows the growth of GDP in real terms in the UK.

Third, many businesses have found that they can access larger markets by exporting. Finding and competing successfully in international markets has brought business success for many. But it can be risky. Businesses have to be able to undertake appropriate market research and assess the potential of the markets they are considering before investing heavily. Figure 7 shows how rising output and incomes can be linked to increased exports for the world as a whole.

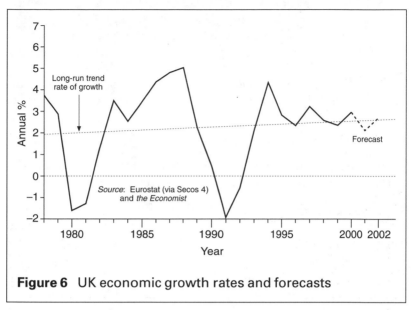

Figure 6 UK economic growth rates and forecasts

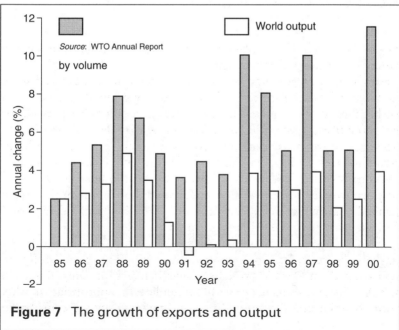

Figure 7 The growth of exports and output

Long-term growth

In the long run, economic growth depends upon an increase in capacity across a wide range of businesses. If businesses are to have an incentive to increase capacity, there must be growing demand for the product. Some of the growing demand comes from the domestic economy, some from exports. You can see that the long-run trend rate of growth has increased slightly in the UK in Figure 6.

Increasing capacity is associated with three important trends in the economy. All three help to increase **productivity**, which means output per person employed:

- rising **investment**, which means more capital per person employed

- improved education and training, which increases human capital – the skills and competences and the flexibility of people

- technological change, which can increase the efficiency of machines and lead to better ways of managing production.

There are some uncertainties about the increase in productivity in recent years. It is generally thought that the use of computers and IT in business has increased productivity greatly. However, some evidence is emerging which suggests that, in the period 2000–2001, the benefits of this may have been somewhat overestimated. Recent data from the US may help to illuminate the issue.

New knowledge and new technologies offer exciting opportunities for some businesses. But there are risks. The banks which were the first to set up Internet access for their customers generally did rather well. Internet shopping presents a much more mixed picture. Tesco made it work while other supermarkets experienced difficulties. Some Internet suppliers found that delivery costs were much higher than anticipated and made losses as a result. Again, keep an eye on the news to see how this type of business is developing.

The business cycle

It is clear from Figure 6 that economic growth is far from steady. There are two important reasons for this.

- One reason is that there is a cycle of **boom, recession, slump** and **recovery** which has existed ever since the industrial revolution. As a result of this the level of activity in the economy fluctuates.

- The other reason is that government policies can influence the level of activity in the economy. If the right policy is not implemented at the right time, the result can be destabilizing.

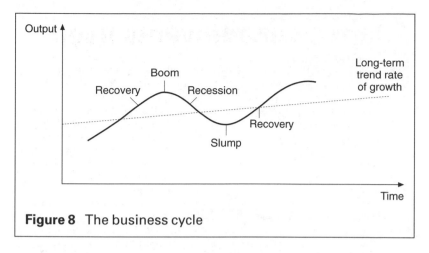

Figure 8 The business cycle

Figure 8 shows a stylized version of the business cycle. During the boom, the economy is growing faster than the trend rate of growth. Rapid growth like this is not sustainable. In time there will be a downturn and the economy will go into recession, which means that output grows more slowly than before. Sometimes output actually decreases. You can see this in Figure 6 in the years 1980/81 and also 1991/92. This means that there is a depression or slump.

Weaker businesses will often come to the end of the road in a recession or a slump. Low levels of profitability turn to losses – and if these appear likely to be permanent, the creditors will close in.

The impact of recession

There is huge variation in the extent to which businesses are vulnerable to the fluctuations of the business cycle. Car manufacturers tend to be vulnerable. If people can postpone buying when their incomes are falling, they will. Producers of basic food items tend to find demand steadier over the years.

Advertizing is an indicator of impending recession. Once demand starts to fall, many businesses reassess their investment plans. Will they need the extra capacity? Many projects will be cancelled. What then happens to the producers of investment goods, the engineering industries and construction businesses?

Typically, lack of demand causes employers to lay off some workers. They then experience falling incomes. At this point in the cycle, the experience of recession becomes much more general. Falling incomes mean falling demand for a wide range of consumer goods. Output may begin to fall as a slump develops. Unemployment rises further.

Advertizers feel the pinch

The level of advertizing is closely linked to the business cycle. Big advertizers spend less when their profits are falling. In fact, advertizing is one of the best indicators of approaching recession. Advertizing growth started to decline in June 2000. At that time the economy was strong. By December 2000, year-on-year growth was down to 2.8%. Early in 2001, several big spenders actually cut their advertizing budgets. Between January and April 2001, Procter & Gamble, specialists in cleaning and washing products, cut spending by 3%. Spending by BT went down by 30%.

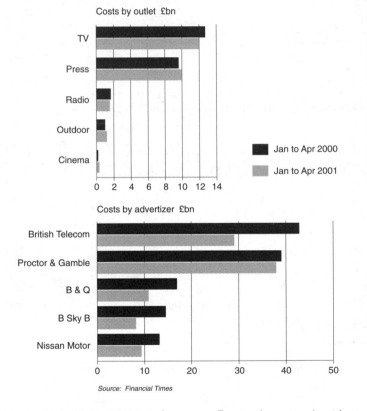

Source: Financial Times

ITV was badly hit by this loss of revenue. Press, cinema and outdoor advertizing benefited as businesses looked for cheaper alternatives to TV and radio. Carlton and Capital Radio announced profits warnings. Some of the lost advertizing reflects the problems of the dotcoms.

Falling demand means less revenue and rigorous cost cutting for the media businesses which suffer.

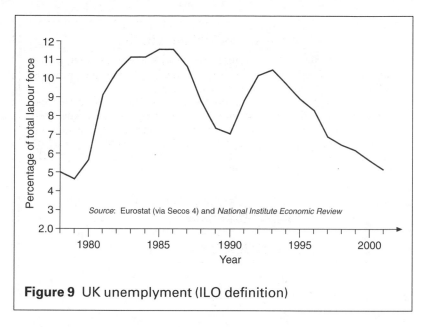

Figure 9 UK unemplyment (ILO definition)

Working out what is happening in recession is made more difficult by the fact that there are time lags. Employers don't like to lay off valued employees, so they wait for as long as they can. Only when they are sure that demand will not improve for some time do they start to make people redundant.

If you compare Figure 9 with Figure 6, you can see that when output was actually falling fastest, unemployment was still fairly low. Equally, as the economy recovers, jobs open up quite slowly. Employers want to be quite sure that demand is increasing before they take on more people.

Phases of the business cycle

Each phase of the business cycle has different features. As you have seen, recession is characterized by slower growth of demand and output, and falling profits. As the economy goes into a slump, output actually falls and unemployment rises. Table 4 shows how the cycle develops.

A serious slump can drag on, because lack of confidence and low levels of consumer demand make businesses very wary about expanding. Eventually though, some businesses find that they have to invest because their equipment is wearing out. Other businesses may find they can expand into export markets which are less depressed. This

Table 4 The business cycle

	Recession	Slump	Recovery	Boom
Output	Growing slowly	Falling	Growing slowly	Growing fast
Employment	High but falling	Low	Low but rising	High
Skill shortages	Diminishing	None	Few	Numerous
Inflation	Slowing	Slowing further	Stable	Accelerating
Confidence	Low and falling	Very low	Improving	High
Investment	Falling	Very low	Growing slowly	Growing fast

will create some demand for investment goods and bring about some expansion of output.

Recovery

Once jobs are being created and unemployment starts to fall, recovery poses few problems. The general air of increased optimism creates easier trading conditions. Problems start to appear as the economy comes closer to full employment. At that point some businesses find that they are unable to recruit people with scarce skills – there are **skills shortages**. Sometimes businesses can recruit, but only by paying higher wages. They may need to do this anyway just to keep key people from leaving.

As wage costs begin to rise, businesses will try to pass on the increase in the form of higher prices to customers. This is the beginning of accelerating inflation. As the labour market tightens, all employers find that pay increases become larger. Excess demand for labour simply pushes up rates of pay.

If growth rates continue to rise, more and more labour will be required. If businesses continue to recruit by giving pay rises and raising prices, we say that the growth rate is *unsustainable*. At that point it will be above the long-run trend rate of growth. Normally, monetary policy will be used to slow the economy down. (This will be covered in Chapter 4.) At this point, the restrictions on growth can be considerable and the economy may proceed into recession. However, in recent years inflation has become less of a problem.

The international dimension

So far, the analysis has been all in terms of the domestic economy. In practice, though, international trade is so important in most economies that it is hardly possible to investigate events without looking at export markets and **exchange rates**.

Recession makes many businesses more energetic about seeking out export markets. It does happen that recession can affect many economies at the same time. When it does, competition intensifies as more businesses chase a diminishing band of customers. However, usually there are at least variations in growth rates which provide openings for increased exports. Figure 10 shows how the UK growth rate compared with those of its two most important trading partners.

Equally, during a boom export efforts are usually diminished – it is so easy to sell on the home market. But wherever the economy is in the business cycle, the state of the exchange rate may have a big impact and change the pattern of events.

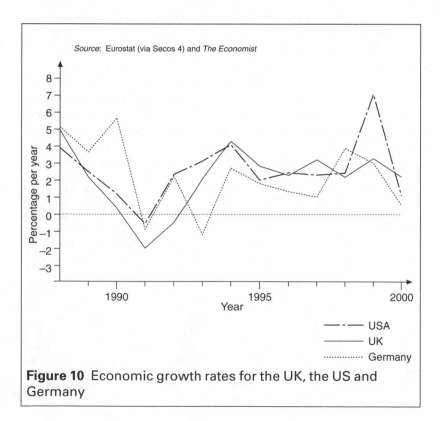

Figure 10 Economic growth rates for the UK, the US and Germany

Exchange rates and business

What exporters want is a nice low exchange rate. This makes it much easier for them to compete. A 15 per cent drop in the exchange rate can work wonders for their competitive position. A rising exchange rate is bad news. Over a period of one to two years a 15 per cent rise might cause an exporting business to lose many of its foreign customers.

Looking at data for exports and exchange rates helps us to see the connections. Table 5 tracks UK export volumes and the effective exchange rate index. The latter is a measure of exchange rate change. It is calculated from a weighted average of the changes in the exchange rate against those of major trading partners.

From 1990 to 1992, the pound was joined up to the European Exchange Rate Mechanism (ERM), which was a forerunner of EMU. However, it had joined at rather a high rate for reasons connected with the control of inflation. This rate was widely expected to be unsustainable and the result was serious speculation against the pound. In late 1992, the then Conservative government decided that the pound should drop out of the ERM and the pound fell immediately, as shown in the 1993 figure in Table 5. It stayed relatively low until 1996, after which problems in Asia led to the pound rising against Asian currencies in which there was little confidence.

The effect on exports of this boost to competitiveness is very clear. Export volumes tend to rise anyway, year by year, as international trade increases. But from 1994 until 1997 exports rose very healthily,

Table 5 UK exports and exchange rates

	Sterling effective exchange rate 1994 = 100	Export volume 1994 = 100
1991	113.0	85
1992	108.7	88
1993	99.7	93
1994	100	100
1995	95.1	110
1996	96.7	118
1997	112.7	128
1998	116.5	129
1999	116.3	133
2000	120.8	146

Source: *National Institute Economic Review*

Psion

Shares in Psion, the handheld computer company, yesterday lost 29% of their value after the group warned that its full-year profit would fall 'well below' analysts' expectations.

Like other companies, Psion has been hit by higher prices for memory components, which are in short supply. It has also seen its margins crumble, hit by the double whammy of the strong dollar, which has driven up purchasing costs, and the ailing euro, which has simultaneously reduced the value of its sales.

The Independent, 28 October 2000

showing a link to the fall in the exchange rate. (Notice that there is a time lag between an exchange rate change and a change in exports.) The subsequent rise in the exchange rate hurt UK manufacturers badly in 1998/99.

Not all businesses are exporters. Exchange rates have different effects on different businesses. What happens to importers if the exchange rate rises? Tea bag manufacturers will get more foreign currency for their pounds and pay less for their tea. Importers of fancy French cheeses will pay less too. Travel agencies will be able to sell more holidays abroad.

Some businesses get around the problem of unpredictable exchange rates by locating production in countries where they have large markets. But then they have to look at the costs in that location, in comparison to others they might choose. The choice is often difficult.

Market access

The gradual opening up of world markets has had a big impact on many businesses, not all of them the large ones. Foreign markets create opportunities. Three important trends are visible.

- The development of the EU has provided numerous opportunities. The EU is not yet a fully integrated single market, but many businesses have been able to expand into EU markets.

- The World Trade Organization has slowly and over many years of negotiation made trade cheaper and easier. Manufacturers have benefited from lower tariffs. In 1996, 50 per cent of the UK's vehicle production was exported, as was 60 per cent of the output of the chemical industry.

● Technological advances create unique and specialized products which have world-wide markets.

Interesting times

From the mid-1990s, the UK economy performed rather well. This is clear from Figure 6 (page 27). But in 1997, the Asian financial crisis hit many of the UK's important markets in the Far East. Businesses sold yen and other Asian currencies and bought pounds which looked safer. This put UK manufacturers in a difficult position. Demand in some of their markets became very depressed and they lost competitiveness. Figure 11 shows what was happening in 1998.

In the meantime, the UK economy carried on growing because the service sector was doing just fine. Worries about inflation kept interest rates high, which did not suit the beleaguered manufacturers. The UK appeared to be developing a two-speed economy.

As the effects of the Asian financial crisis subsided, many people wondered whether the business cycle was dead. The UK and the US had had steady growth for eight years. But trouble was round the corner.

By 2001 there were serious worries about the US economy; growth

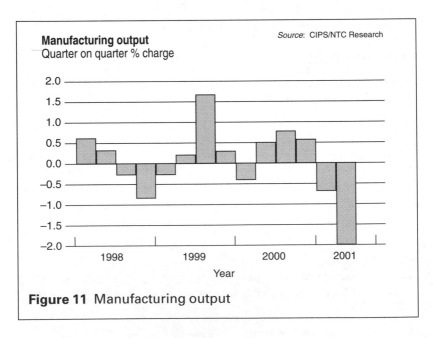

Figure 11 Manufacturing output

was slowing after the long buoyant period. The Japanese economy remained sluggish after several poor years. Readers must find out for themselves what happened next in the world's major economies.

KEY WORDS

Structural change	Recession
Productivity	Slump
Investment	Recovery
Business cycle	Skills shortages
Boom	Exchange rates

Further reading

Ingham, G., *Managing Change: A Guide to British Economic Policy*, Manchester University Press, 2000.

Marcouse, I. *et al.*, Unit 62 in *Business Studies*, Hodder & Stoughton, 1999.

Mason, T., 'Rover Cars: the end of the road?' *Business Review*, February 2001.

The Economist, Chapters 3 and 4 in *Guide to Economic Indicators*, 4th edn, Economist Newspaper Ltd, 2000.

Useful websites

• The site of the Office of National Statistics has good data: www.statistics.gov.uk.

• Find out what is happening in the economy by searching the newspaper websites. The *Financial Times* has the best search facility though the articles may be complex: www.ft.com. You can put the name of any newspaper into a search engine such as Google. You will need to search carefully when you get there – don't put in <business cycle> because you will get sites on bikes.

• The BBC is useful for the news of the day: www.bbc.co.uk.

Essay topic

Explain how a recession may affect (a) a manufacturer of firelighters, and (b) a high-class chain of restaurants. Suggest three possible strategies which might be adopted to deal with any difficulties. Evaluate the likely possible success of each of the three strategies.

Data response question

Read this piece which is reproduced from the *Financial Times* of 10 September 2001. Then answer the questions that follow.

PC revenues 'set to fall by 10%'

Manufacturers of personal computers will see revenues fall by more than 10% this year owing to a combination of weak demand and falling prices, according to a gloomy new forecast from International Data Corporation, the market research company.

IDC is expecting global unit sales of PCs to fall by 1.6% to about 130 million during 2001. As recently as June the company was forecasting unit growth of 5.8%. The revised forecast underscores the challenge faced by PC makers accustomed to double-digit growth in demand for their products.

Hewlett-Packard last week agreed to pay $20 billion for rival PC maker Compaq, a deal which would create the world's largest manufacturer. The two companies have promised to strip costs from their combined PC operation in an effort to improve margins.

Gateway, another top-tier US PC manufacturer, last month announced a restructuring plan including the closure of its European and Asian operations.

For 2002, IDC is predicting a recovery in sales. However, pricing pressure is expected to continue. As a result, revenues are expected to decline by a further 2%.

Pricing pressure is particularly intense in the US where Dell has been cutting prices in an effort to build market share. Dell, which sells directly to customers through its website and telephone sales operation, is currently the largest PC manufacturer and the industry's lowest cost producer.

Dell's chief financial officer told investors that the company was unlikely to use acquisitions to increase its share of the PC market despite the challenge posed by the combination of HP and Compaq.

1. Why was demand for computers weak in 2001?   [1 mark]
2. Explain the impact of weak demand on the industry.   [3 marks]
3. What assumptions was IDC making in forecasting a recovery in sales in 2002?   [3 marks]
4. Do you think it likely that this recovery actually occurred? Give your reasons.   [4 marks]

5. The day after this report was written, terrorists destroyed the World Trade Center in New York. In what ways may this have affected PC manufacturers subsequently? [4 marks]

6. Evaluate the extent to which PC manufacturers are vulnerable to fluctuations in demand resulting from the business cycle. [5 marks]

Chapter Four

Macroeconomic policy

'A nation's economic role is to improve its citizens' standard of living by enhancing the value of what they contribute to the world economy.'
Robert Reich, in *The Work of Nations* (1991)

The term 'macroeconomic policy' includes all the ways in which governments try to influence what happens in the economy as a whole. Government objectives will usually be a combination of two or more of the four major areas for action:

● economic growth

● unemployment

● inflation

● trade.

The tools of macroeconomic policy include **fiscal policy, monetary policy** and **exchange rate policy**. These categories take in most of what governments want to do to influence the economy.

There are other related policies which can be made into a package of measures. This may be more effective than relying on a single policy. For example, a government which is seeking to encourage economic growth might well try to reduce the amount of red tape which businesses have to contend with and also to attract foreign investment. The former is not, strictly speaking, a macroeconomic policy but it could be a useful part of a policy package (if it actually happens).

Politics

Macroeconomic policy can be very controversial. Government and opposition may well have quite different proposals. In recent years some areas of agreement have emerged, in the UK and in other countries.

In spite of this, some governments are more 'interventionist' than others. While a 'laissez faire' government would probably expect **interest rates** to be used to control spending, it would be unlikely to raise tax rates, at least most of the time, and might try to limit the scope of government action. In contrast, an interventionist government might make considerable adjustments to tax rates and introduce a range of measures to help specific industries. A very active interventionist approach is currently out of fashion. Nevertheless, the Chancellor, Gordon Brown, has a reputation for 'tinkering' with policy. In the past, the UK government would have had a big say in the setting of interest rates. Nowadays the **Bank of England** makes the decision. This means that a significant element of economic policy is now kept out of politics altogether.

Monetary policy

Monetary policy in practice means changes in interest rates. The Bank of England does do other things as well, but all are geared towards reinforcing its control over interest rates. It uses interest rates to influence the level of spending in the economy so that it can control the rate of inflation. The actual rate set by the Bank of England is known as the base rate. Inflation can have damaging effects on the economy because it is destabilizing and unpredictable.

Figure 12 shows how interest rates have changed in response to problems with inflation. Because interest rates are set with an inflation target in mind, and because inflation tends to accelerate in a boom, evidence of booming markets will usually cause the Bank of England to raise its rates.

Similarly, a low rate of inflation and evidence of recession will encourage the Bank to cut interest rates. It will want to help businesses which face falling demand and falling profits.

The government's economic policy objectives

The government's central economic objective is to achieve high and stable levels of growth and employment. Price stability is a precondition for these high and stable levels of growth and employment, which will in turn help to create the conditions for price stability on a sustainable basis. In the recent past, instability has contributed to the UK's poor growth performance, not least by holding back the long-term investment that is the foundation for a successful economy.

The monetary policy objectives of the Bank of England are to maintain price stability and, subject to that, to support the government's economic policy, including its objectives for growth and employment.

Source: Remit for the Monetary Policy Committee, presented by Gordon Brown, June 1998.

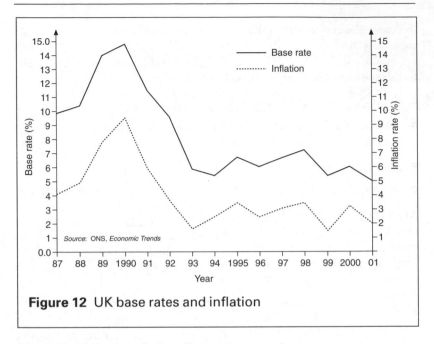

Figure 12 UK base rates and inflation

How the Monetary Policy Committee works

The actual decisions about the base rate are taken every month by the Monetary Policy Committee (MPC) of the Bank of England. There are usually eight members, with the governor of the Bank in the chair. Of the members, some will be from the staff of the Bank, others will be outsiders, usually economists with a distinguished track record in the City or a university.

Manufacturing relief

Manufacturers around the country greeted yesterday's quarter-point cut in interest rates with relief. Scottish industry was delighted with the cut, which comes a day after official figures showed a 2% fall in Scottish manufacturing output during the first quarter, a second successive quarterly contraction.

'Manufacturing is in recession, and this quarter-point reduction is a welcome relief,' said Peter Hughes, chief executive of Scottish Engineering. 'No one in the manufacturing engineering sector is daft enough to think that this cut on its own will cure the ills of the industry – but it's certainly a cut in the right direction.'

Financial Times, 3 August 2001

The evidence the MPC takes into account includes:

- demand and output in the economy as a whole
- the growth of lending by banks
- the state of the world economy
- whether the labour market is tight with skill shortages and many vacancies, or unemployment is growing
- prices and costs of production
- retail spending and house prices.

After the monthly meeting a press announcement is made. The base rate may or may not be changed. In the event that the base rate is increased, there is a rise in the rate of interest which the Bank of England charges the banks when they borrow from it (which they regularly do). They will then have to pass this increase on to their customers in the form of higher interest rates on loans and overdrafts. This means that interest rates throughout the economy will rise. The reverse happens for a rate cut.

Figure 13 shows how the base rate moved over a two-year period. In 1999, demand for manufactures was very sluggish, but then worries

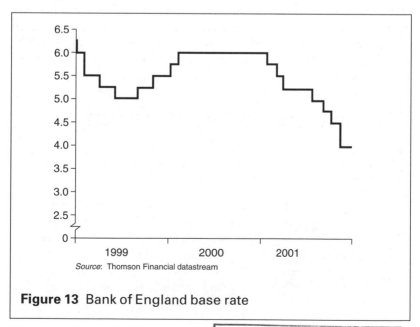

Figure 13 Bank of England base rate

about possible inflation developed. By 2001 there were anxieties about a possible recession, perhaps spreading from the US.

The impact of interest rate changes

Interest rates affect consumers who are buying with credit, homeowners with mortgages, and businesses with bank loans. Higher base rates mean that everyone has to pay more for their loans. They thus have an incentive to borrow less. This means they will spend less. Reduced consumer spending will mean reduced demand for many products. Some businesses will cancel or postpone their investment and expansion plans. Demand for equipment and buildings will fall. There may be some redundancies.

After a while, employers will not need to pay high wages to attract the labour they require, so cost pressures will be less and there will be fewer price rises. There may be some price cuts. The rise in interest rates will reduce the rate of inflation. With luck and good management, inflation will be fended off without depressing economic activity too much. Economic growth will be kept at a sustainable level. This is what seemed to be happening during the late 1990s.

Monetary policy in recession

In recession, as demand falters, business becomes less profitable. If losses are made, firms will start by increasing their bank loans to cover the difference. If the situation continues, the solution may be to contract output and make the jobs of some people redundant.

Contracting output means that some incomes will be falling and demand overall will fall further. The economy can go into a downward spiral as the effects of reduced demand are passed on from one sector to another.

In these circumstances, a cut in interest rates will reduce the pressure on businesses and help them to avoid bankruptcy. They may make fewer people redundant and replace their worn-out equipment rather than close down. The impact of recession will be reduced. Figure 14 shows the sequence of events.

The whole situation is complicated by the fact that changes in interest rates affect the economy with a time lag. It can take two years for a cut in interest rates to have a visible impact in terms of increasing demand in the economy. However, individual businesses will usually feel the benefit, in terms of their costs, sooner than that. It can take longer for the change to filter through into actual decisions.

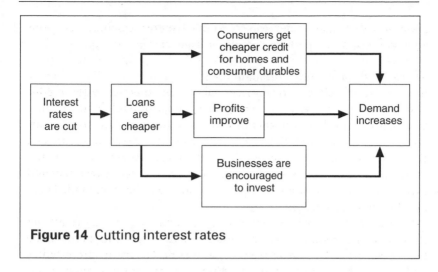

Figure 14 Cutting interest rates

Business decisions under monetary policy

When big decisions have to be made, businesses have to be very much aware of possible interest rate changes and their likely impact. Large businesses will employ people to forecast future developments for them. Sometimes decisions are affected not so much by actual events as by business confidence about the future. This is not always accurate and it may itself have a bad effect. Lack of confidence may reduce spending and itself contribute to recession. Bad news from individual companies may influence business confidence considerably.

Fiscal policy

Fiscal policy covers all kinds of taxes and government expenditures. While monetary policy has to a large extent ceased to be a political

---

Cisco gives a profits warning

Cisco is the world's largest networking equipment provider. Early in 2001 it announced a sharp fall in sales revenue, down 30 per cent on the previous quarter, and the shedding of 25 per cent of the workforce. The chief executive blamed the economic slowdown in the US, but added that demand was weak in Asia, particularly Korea, Taiwan, Australia and Japan. Excess inventories would have to be written off and some facilities would be closed down.

An interest rate cut can cushion the effect of changes in demand like the one described here.

football, fiscal policy remains very much a matter of debate.

Fiscal policy can be used to influence activity in the economy. A tax cut will increase disposable income and lead to people spending more. There will be increased demand and many businesses will benefit. Equally, if the economy is working flat out and there are worries about inflation, a tax increase will help to slow things down.

Most people persist in wanting to have better public services and lower taxes. In practice this is usually impossible to achieve. In the past twenty years in the UK the emphasis has tended to be on tax cuts, as a politically popular measure. If taxes have already been cut, public services may be threatened. It may be difficult to cut taxes further, even though it would help to reduce the impact of recession on businesses and people.

Equally, the economy may well benefit from a tax increase if spending is already at a high level. But if the government promised not to increase taxes at the last election, this may be tricky.

Government borrowing

Governments may borrow more in a recession. This allows them to increase government expenditure while keeping tax rates the same or even cutting them. Tax revenue will fall anyway in a recession because incomes and profits are falling. You can see how this worked in the case study on the early 1990s shown in the box.

The annual amount of government borrowing is called the *public sector net cash requirement*, shown in Figure 15. You can see how it is linked to the business cycle if you compare this chart with that in Chapter 3 (Figure 6, page 27).

A slump in the early 1990s

The recession of the early 1990s had a very major impact on the world economy. In the UK, output fell by 2.5 per cent between 1990 and 1992. Unemployment rose to 10.5 per cent in 1993 (because of time lags). Both manufacturing and services were hit. Bankruptcies went from 8000 in 1989 to a peak of 32 000 in 1992. The government both cut taxes and increased expenditure. Borrowing increased substantially to fund an increase in spending which probably helped to bring recession to an end.

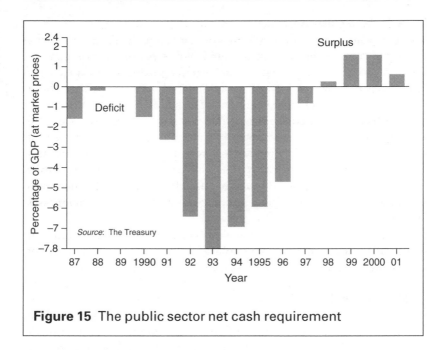

Figure 15 The public sector net cash requirement

Exchange rate policy

In practice, it is difficult to analyse monetary and fiscal policy without taking account of exchange rates and the trade situation. Businesses are very much affected by exchange rates and they can reinforce changes brought about by the business cycle (this was dealt with in Chapter 3).

Interest rates actually have their impact on businesses partly through the exchange rate. A rise in interest rates attracts capital from abroad, and this inflow will increase the demand for pounds. This will push up the exchange rate, making imports cheaper and exports dearer. The international competitiveness of many businesses will be reduced.

Since 1997, the UK exchange rate has generally been rather high and many manufacturing businesses have found this to be a real problem (see Table 5 in Chapter 3). It might have been possible to bring the exchange rate down by reducing interest rates. But monetary policy was directed towards dealing with inflationary tendencies, so the MPC did not want to do this. These inflationary tendencies were more evident in south-east England than elsewhere and northern manufacturers complained vigorously.

A floating exchange rate

Governments can in theory choose between fixed and **floating exchange rates**. If they are fixed, they will be tied to another currency, such as the US dollar. Some Latin American countries do this. It can bring greater stability to an economy.

The UK has had a floating exchange rate since 1972. This means that there is some flexibility: there are times when it is possible for the Bank of England to encourage a lower exchange rate, providing a gain in competitiveness. In theory it can sell pounds, thus bringing the price down. The gain in competitiveness leads to better export prospects. The downside is that a floating exchange rate may be unstable and unpredictable. Also, a falling exchange rate can encourage inflation because it makes imports dearer.

Economic and Monetary Union

There is an alternative to a floating exchange rate, but it does involve some loss of independence in policy matters for both the government and the central bank. **The Economic and Monetary Union** (EMU) of the EU has twelve members – all the EU in fact except Sweden, Denmark and the UK. Sweden may join soon. If the UK joined, the pound would go and businesses would no longer have to contend with a fluctuating exchange rate between the pound and the euro. Government policy is that before joining, the UK must satisfy the five economic tests set out by Gordon Brown (see the box).

There is room for debate on the five economic tests. In any case, on EMU, business splits down the middle. The chief executive officers (CEOs) of Granada and Northern Foods, for example, are well-known supporters and there are many others. But a survey of manufacturers by the Engineering Employers Federation in early 2001 found:

The Chancellor's five economic tests

- Will the UK be able to adjust to euro interest rates?
- Is there sufficient flexibility to cope with economic change?
- What will be the effect on long-term investment in the UK?
- What will be the impact on our financial services industry?
- Will the euro be good for growth, stability and employment?

- 21 per cent in favour
- 14 per cent against
- 29 per cent supportive in principle
- 36 per cent saying 'wait and see'.

Many people in business would like the certainty associated with using the same currency throughout the EU. Others put a higher priority on preserving the right of the UK government to decide its own monetary policy.

A likely possible outcome of EMU is transparent pricing throughout the euro-zone. Any variations in prices in different countries will be easily visible to consumers because they will all be stated in euros. It will be possible to shop around across national borders. Some businesses will find this intensifies the competition they face. They may not like it, but consumers seem likely to benefit.

So do we trust these bankers?

The arguments for British membership relate chiefly to the cost of dealing with fluctuating exchange rates. Supporters also say that the longer Britain stays out, the more likely it is that multinationals will look abroad, inward investment will dry up and thousands of British jobs will be lost.

Alternatively, how can a one-size-fits-all economic policy work across the eurozone's twelve countries? This could remain an issue even if the five economic tests were met.

But what evidence do we have that these imbalances would be any worse than the impact of Bank of England decisions on Merseyside shipyards? What makes the difference in the UK is that people are more likely to get on their bikes from depressed areas to booming ones such as Cambridge than they are to seek work in Cologne. And if there are serious regional imbalances, the UK government has the power to spend proportionately more money on the needy regions – as it does in Northern Ireland.

That is the nub, say anti-euro campaigners. For the euro to work, Europe needs such transfers of spending, which eventually means stronger European government. Either way, it is a political question.

The Observer, 20 May 2001

What's been happening?

UK businesses have had very varied experiences in recent years. The service sector has had much easier trading conditions than manufacturing. In general, the different sectors of the economy present very different conditions.

Whatever the government's policies, a number of trends are discernible:

- the pattern of demand changes

- growth rates vary between regions and industries

- new technologies lead to promising development but also to labour-saving investment which reduces the number of jobs.

One way to look at the changes is to study the unemployment data. Regional unemployment rates still differ, and there have been striking shifts in the pattern of employment between industries (see Figure 16).

Because of these variations, macroeconomic policy generally has limitations in relation to unemployment. Training and tax and benefit incentives can be more appropriate measures. These and other measures can be built into policy packages alongside the macroeconomic policies.

Businesses must constantly monitor the environment in which they operate and any possible policy changes, before taking decisions. Failure to consider the effects of economic policy can lead to bad decisions.

KEY WORDS	
Economic growth	Exchange rate policy
Unemployment	Interest rates
Inflation	The Bank of England
Trade	Floating exchange rates
Fiscal policy	Economic and Monetary Union
Monetary policy	

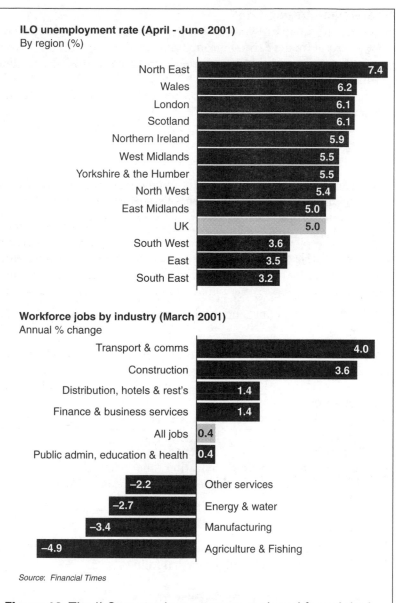

ILO unemployment rate (April - June 2001)
By region (%)

Region	%
North East	7.4
Wales	6.2
London	6.1
Scotland	6.1
Northern Ireland	5.9
West Midlands	5.5
Yorkshire & the Humber	5.5
North West	5.4
East Midlands	5.0
UK	5.0
South West	3.6
East	3.5
South East	3.2

Workforce jobs by industry (March 2001)
Annual % change

Industry	%
Transport & comms	4.0
Construction	3.6
Distribution, hotels & rest's	1.4
Finance & business services	1.4
All jobs	0.4
Public admin, education & health	0.4
Other services	−2.2
Energy & water	−2.7
Manufacturing	−3.4
Agriculture & Fishing	−4.9

Source: *Financial Times*

Figure 16 The ILO unemployment rate and workforce jobs by industry, UK.

Further reading
Gillespie, A., Chapter 4 in *Competitive Environment and External Influences*, Hodder & Stoughton, 2000.

Jewell, B., Chapter 11 in *An Integrated Approach to Business Studies*, 4th edn, Longman, 2000.

Smith, D., *UK Current Economic Policy*, Heinemann Educational, 1999.

The Economist Guide to Economic Indicators, 2000.

Useful websites

- To gain a comprehensive understanding of the impact of monetary and fiscal policies, go to the Virtual Economy at www.bized.ac.uk. Click on 'Virtual Worlds' and then 'Virtual Economy'. Try your hand at being Chancellor.

- For an overview of current data, go to the Treasury's most recent data site: www.treasury.gov.uk/e_info/overview/b2.html.

- For detail on the most recent UK budget, try Deloitte Touche's site, www.UKBudget.com, and look for the economic review of the budget.

- For more information on the euro, try the Association for Monetary Union of Europe: www.amue.org.

Essay topics
1. Examine the likely effects on a business you have studied of the UK joining the euro.
2. What policies might governments use to reduce the impact of recession on businesses? Selecting one particular business or industry, evaluate the likely impact of the measures which may be used.

Data response question
Read the following account of one person's attempt to start a small business. Then answer the questions that follow.

Anita's House

In late 1997, Anita decided to give up her job as a chef working in a big city-centre restaurant and open up on her own. She moved to a small town near Manchester where she could rent suitable premises. She set up in business as Anita's House, offering a high-quality menu based on traditional French dishes and modern British cooking. Before very long, she was noticed by potential customers from her own and neighbouring towns and villages. She built up a clientele of generally fairly young professionals who were themselves prospering. They were prepared to drive to get to her restaurant, and word of the quality of her cooking spread. Advertizing executives and media people generally, people working in the financial sector and some local business people liked the style and saw the food as good value for money compared with competing restaurants.

By early 2001, the question of expansion had inevitably come up. Anita's kitchen space was cramped for the type of cooking she did. The restaurant was fully booked every night, usually more than a week in advance. The premises next door came on the market. However, substantial borrowing would be necessary if Anita was to have a chance of buying. Then more finance would be needed to run the two buildings together, expand the kitchen and decorate.

For some years, incomes had been growing in the area. Three pleasant new housing estates had been built within a five-mile radius. However, there were stories of local manufacturing businesses having to make people redundant because of the high pound. There was talk of recession in the US. It seemed a long way away but it was in every newspaper. There was also a rumour that a well-known chain of up-market restaurants was considering setting up nearby.

Anita saw that decisions could no longer be put off.

1. Outline four possible options for Anita's business. [4 marks]
2. What information will Anita need in order to help her decide between the various options? How should she set about getting it? [3 marks]
3. Explain the pros and cons of each of the options you have identified. [4 marks]
4. Select the option which in your view made the best sense at the time, giving a full explanation for your decision. [4 marks]
5. Assuming that Anita followed your plan, and knowing what happened to the business environment in the UK after the time of the decision, explain what you think would have happened to Anita's business in the years which followed. [5 marks]

Chapter Five

Technical change

'If a man write a better book, preach a better sermon, or make a better mouse-trap than his neighbour, tho' he build a house in the woods, the world will make a beaten path to his door.'
Ralph Waldo Emerson, 1803–1882

'Technology' means the application of science to production processes. So technical change means the use of new technologies, producing in ways which were previously impossible or too costly.

Just being able to do something does not necessarily make it practical or possible. We know how to put men on the moon. But more than thirty years after the first successful landing, we don't bother to try because the benefits of going there are far outweighed by the cost at the present time. The US government, which could make a different choice, buys fighter planes, medical care for elderly people on low incomes and scientific research in outer space, but not manned flights to the moon.

Most technical change happens because there is a commercial incentive – someone can make a profit by doing things differently. The bigger the potential profit, the greater the incentive to invest in a new development.

Some technical changes happen because governments or non-profit-making organizations are willing to pay for them. Some medical

Robo Chop

If you'd rather lie in a hammock sipping beer than push a lawnmower, your prayers may have been answered by the Robomower. *Gardening Which?* researchers took this robotic mower for a spin, and were pretty impressed.

After pegging down a low-voltage perimeter wire around the edge of your lawn (level with the soil surface),
you're ready to go. Robomower trundles automatically over your lawn chopping your grass to your chosen height. Bumper sensors redirect it when it hits an object, and the signals from the perimeter wire prevent it from mowing your flower beds.

At £750, whether it appeals to you will really depend on the size of your lawn and the size of your wallet.

Which?, June 2001

research falls into this category. Even then there may be strong cost-based motives. For example, it was well worth it for the National Health Service to perfect aspects of keyhole surgery because it reduced the cost of some operations. It might have been worthwhile even without that incentive if it helped people to get better faster.

Technical change and innovation

Innovation means using new technologies to develop new products or new processes. The outcome is increased efficiency – more output without necessarily having to increase inputs. Often innovation provides new and better ways to add value.

In practice, many product developments are improvements rather than brand new products. You might have seen a 1930s washing machine in a museum. In theory the washing machine is not now a new product, but in practice there is no comparison between the old and the present-day versions. In this case, **product innovation** is occurring during the design process, as well as in the engineering of the product.

Process innovation is in many ways just as important as product innovation. Because it is all about cutting costs of production, it can lead to lower prices. When consumers can get their desired products for less, their incomes will go further and their standards of living rise. This outcome can be achieved when new types of machinery and equipment are invented. But organizing production in better ways is important too in process innovation. Cell production, just-in-time stock control and de-layering can facilitate process innovation by making the organization more flexible.

Many products have been revolutionized by **CAD/CAM**. This stands for *computer-assisted design and computer-aided manufacturing*. These lead, respectively, to product and process innovation. Further innovations in the programming of these systems will bring more changes in the future.

Product innovation

We can see product innovation happening all around us. Mobile phones provide a recent example. They have come a long way from the original 'brick'. Many people who have them would say that they have contributed to the adoption of a new and improved lifestyle.

Perhaps even more significantly, product innovation can contribute to resolving difficult social and environmental problems. A rash of new distance-learning MBAs have brought business education to countless people whose incomes would not have permitted them to attend courses on a full-time basis. This is just one example of a service

Which way to the hydrogen economy?

For decades, ever since the early fuel cells accompanied man into space, scientists have dreamt of the day when the world would be powered by clean, green hydrogen energy rather than filthy hydrocarbons like petrol. That is because fuel cells take hydrogen and combine it with oxygen from the air to generate electricity. As a result, the only waste produced by these big batteries is water and heat. Many experts have predicted that one day fuel cells will power all our homes, cars and perhaps even mobile phones and laptop computers.

Does all this mean that the hydrogen economy is round the corner? No, is the blunt answer. Fuel cells themselves are close to market reality but there is a snag: the fuel that these wondrous cells run on – hydrogen – is one that the modern industrial economy simply is not organized to deliver. Very few places in the world have pure hydrogen available on demand. The infrastructure will take many years to develop. Yet the purveyors of fuel cells still intend to introduce them to the market soon. How can they possibly power them?

That points to a dirty little secret about fuel cells that neither the fat cats selling them nor the greens heralding them want to talk about – the first generation of fuel cells will use 'transition' fuels that do not live up to the full promise of clean hydrogen energy. If the hydrogen is made by a 'reformer' that consumes hydrocarbon fuels such as petrol, natural gas or methanol, this process will be polluting – though far less so than today's engines and power plants. It is this lack of infrastructure that will dictate the order in which fuel-cell applications will take off: stationary power first, fleet vehicles next and, only later, ordinary cars.

The world's oil giants, aware that some of these choices could well put them out of business one day, have joined the debate. Most of them have entered into partnerships with car firms to develop prototypes and fuel infrastructure. DaimlerChrysler and BP, among others, intend to put dozens of test cars and buses on the roads of California in coming months.

Not so long ago, oilmen were openly mocking the notion that fuel cells could ever replace the internal combustion engine. Now many openly gush about the arrival of the 'Hydrogen Age'. Ultimately, their real concern is that consumers fill up at their fuel-station of the future, whatever fuel is in the pump.

Source: adapted from 'The world in 2001', *The Economist,* 2001 product innovation made much easier by technical change in electronic communications. New products can be deliberately designed to be more environmentally friendly than the ones they are replacing. Sometimes this is a response to legal restrictions. The Californian government has very restrictive requirements about emissions from cars. These have concentrated the minds of vehicle designers because they have only a few years to make the necessary improvements.

Other environmentally friendly products have been brought to the market in the expectation that consumers can be induced to pay more for them. There is a **profit incentive**.

New product development

So far we have looked at how new technologies affect societies and standards of living. But from the point of view of the individual business, new product development is first and foremost a way of coping with competition. If they are able to give their product a unique selling point, they can charge a higher price.

Competition may prompt efforts to improve quality and reliability. Some of the improvements will be realized at the design stage, when carefully tested prototypes lead the way to product improvements.

New product development is risky. A business may invest a huge amount in the development process, only to find that the results are disappointing. So, sometimes, businesses will invest in research and development (R&D) only when the expected profits are large.

Although small businesses do get very much involved in new product development, there are some kinds of research which are just too expensive for small organizations. Pharmaceutical companies spend a lot on R&D. The cost of bringing new drugs to the market, after all the necessary safety tests have been performed, can be prohibitive for smaller businesses. Development requires the backing of a large and strong organization which can afford to spread the risks by working on a number of different new products, some of which will be more successful than others.

Patent protection

A **patent** gives the owner of a new invention the right to be the sole supplier of it for a given length of time, often ten years. This allows the cost of developing the product to be recouped by charging a price that is greater than the actual costs of production.

Without patents, there would be much less incentive to develop new products. It would be difficult for innovative people and businesses to cover the costs of research and development. There is a large body of patent law, and patent holders have to be prepared to defend their rights in court.

The owners of intellectual property rights include people and businesses which develop new products, authors who write books and those who write or record music. Their rights have to be legally protected if they are to be rewarded in a way which keeps the flow of innovation and creativity going.

The speed of change and the product life-cycle

In recent years the pace of innovation has increased. **Product life-cycles** have to some extent shortened. The forces of competition make it imperative for businesses to innovate on a continuous basis. Unless they do this, they may lose market share to others who have gained a competitive advantage with a new product.

Some new products are flops. Perhaps mini-disks will find a growing market in the future, but to date they have not seriously challenged CDs. The businesses that developed them have had a poor return on their investment. On the other hand, as ways are found to provide a commercial market in Internet recordings, CDs may experience big changes.

'Time to market', the length of time it takes to bring a product from concept to production and distribution, has become a crucial element in the competitive process. Computer-aided design (CAD) has been helpful here because it shortens the lead time. It has become possible for businesses to respond faster to changes in market demand. Again the speed with which they can do this may give them their competitive edge.

One way to make sure that change happens fast enough for the business to stay competitive is to use the concept of continuous improvement, or *kaizen*. This Japanese idea can apply to products or processes. It involves implementing ideas which improve the product or cut costs as and when they occur – not just when production is undergoing a major reorganization.

Process innovation

Cutting costs and increasing efficiency usually mean finding a better way of producing. Here, too, the speed of change has accelerated in the past decade. There are a number of ways in which process innovation may be activated.

- Invest in new types of equipment as it becomes available. They may be more precise or more reliable or just faster.

- Reorganize the production process, for example by bringing in a Kanban system which is computer controlled and uses just-in-time stock control.

- Produce to order rather than in batches, again using computer control.

Process innovation may require that management strategies be equally innovative. There are a number of ways of facilitating technical changes. These are particularly important if the business has become set in its ways and needs to change rapidly in order to survive.

- Reorganize the management structure, perhaps adopting a less hierarchical or bureaucratic system.

- Change the way in which jobs are divided up amongst the workforce, perhaps moving from an assembly line to cell production or a hybrid of the two.

- Encourage multi-skilling so that employees can do a range of different tasks.

- Create closer supplier relationships which improve the quality of inputs.

Continuous improvement can apply to process innovation as well as product innovation. A corporate culture which encourages employees to make suggestions and engage in the planning of production may be conducive to necessary changes.

Quality control can be enhanced by process innovation. New ways can be devised to reduce wastage, correcting faults before they become a real problem. All kinds of process innovation can be used to give businesses a cost advantage over their competing rivals. Process innovation may make them more profitable or it may allow them to cut prices, either of which will strengthen their competitive position.

Increasing productivity

Technical change provides a vitally important element in the process of economic growth. It enables us to get a larger quantity of output from existing quantities of resources. Sometimes we are lucky enough to be able to mobilize more resources. North Sea oil provides an example. Sometimes the increased resources come from investment in production facilities, or infrastructure, such as the Channel tunnel. Often, increasing output and incomes come from using new technologies to innovate.

Dagenham reinvents itself

Assembly workers at Ford's new diesel engine plant in Dagenham, Essex, will be able to shop online and enjoy ultra-flexible working hours to escape travel-to-work congestion and supermarket queues.

The assembly operations will be housed in a 'clean room' featuring a sophisticated air induction and extraction system to minimize airborne dust particles that could damage the new, quiet, fuel-efficient engines.

The plant, part of Ford's strategy to 'reinvent itself', will be built inside a disused building on the 1924-vintage Dagenham estate and will produce 900,000 engines a year by 2004, rising to a potential 1.5 million.

About 400 engineers and support staff, many of them young graduates working alongside older production staff, will be offered a 'better work-life balance' to attract them to the new facility, which will be more akin to a Californian PC plant.

Kevin O'Neill, director of Ford's diesel business in Europe, said: 'An old established site can have the mission of piloting completely new ways of working.'

The Guardian, 14 July 2001

Productivity measures output per person employed. It is a useful way to look at the impact of increased investment and process innovation combined. These are the two ways in which businesses can increase output without necessarily taking on more employees.

UK productivity has not grown particularly fast over the long run, compared with some other countries. Nevertheless, the increases in productivity make a useful contribution to the process of economic growth. During the late 1990s, the UK actually performed well in this respect, though not as well as the US. Table 6 and Figure 17 show the trends.

Table 6 Annual percentage productivity growth in the UK

1988	1989	1990	1991	1992	1993	1994
1.5	−0.2	−0.1	0.3	2.3	3.2	3.6

1995	1996	1997	1998	1999	2000
1.8	1.5	1.5	1.4	1.4	2.3

Source: *National Institute Economic Review*

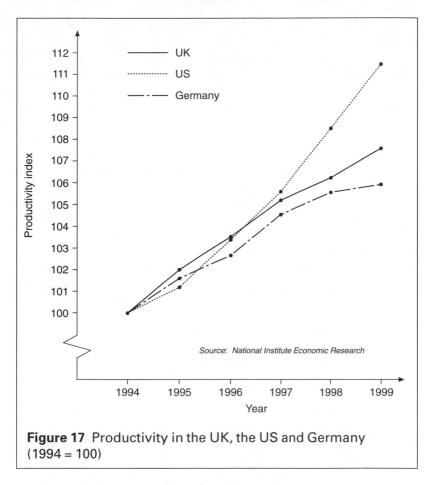

Figure 17 Productivity in the UK, the US and Germany (1994 = 100)

Productivity on a year-by-year basis is influenced by the business cycle. It tends to increase more than usual during the recovery phase, as output increases more than employment. It is also influenced by the level of investment, irrespective of whether that involves technical change. Having more equipment will generally increase an employee's productivity, even though there may be nothing especially innovative about it. It remains the case that technical change and innovation make a major contribution to rising productivity.

Fewer jobs or more?

Some people have come to associate technical change with job losses. It does frequently happen that businesses invest in more and better capital equipment and make some employees redundant. In

61

manufacturing particularly, there has been a big drop in numbers employed.

In spite of this, employment in the UK and in the US grew considerably during the 1990s. As some jobs came to an end in manufacturing, others opened up in the service sector. Some jobs were created in the manufacture of new products, or goods for which demand was increasing.

The increased incomes which come from long-term economic growth give people more spending power and increase demand for a wide range of products. Often these are services – meals out, or tourist and leisure experiences. What technology does do is to make lifetime employment a lot less likely. Figure 16 in Chapter 4 (page 51) gives some indication of the changes.

Resistance to change

In the past, employees have not always made it easy for businesses to innovate. But competition in the labour market and trade union legislation have changed that. Collaborative approaches make wide-ranging changes possible.

Recent research shows that employment relationships in the workplace are now very different from those of the past. People negotiate individually with their employers, rather than collectively through a trade union. Arrangements are much more flexible. Where trade unions do have a significant position, they have sought to collaborate with employers' attempts to innovate, rather than to resist. It has become possible to redesign jobs by negotiation on a local or an individual basis. Ways have been found to survive in the face of strong international competition.

Business success has been greatest where there exists a corporate culture which welcomes change. Where the adjustment process has proved to be too difficult, businesses have tended to merge and lose their old identity in a rationalization process that brought the old ways to an end.

KEY WORDS

Product innovation	Patent
Process innovation	Product life-cycles
CAD/CAM	Productivity
Profit incentive	Resistance to change
New product development	

Further reading

Brooks, I., and Weatherston, J., Chapter 4 in *The Business Environment, Challenges and Changes*, 2nd edn, FT/Prentice Hall, 2000.

Marcouse, I. *et al.* Unit 73 in *Business Studies*, Hodder & Stoughton, 1999.

Scholes, K., 'Information, IT and strategy' in *Teaching Business and Economics*, The Journal of the Economics and Business Education Association, 2001.

Worthington, I., and Britton, C., Chapter 5 in *The Business Environment, Challenges and Changes*, 2nd edn, FT/Prentice Hall, 2000.

Useful websites

- Bized (www.bized.ac.uk) can be used to access a wide range of useful material. Put 'innovation' into the search facility and look for 'Strategy, innovation, technology and competition'. Select the Warwick University site and 'Innovation'. Look for the Overview of Module 1. (It's actually at Brighton University's site but is easier to reach this way.)

- Alternatively, go direct to Warwick University's Business Process Research Centre and select innovation: http://bprc.warwick.ac.uk.rc-inn.html.

Essay topics

1. To what extent is innovation essential to business survival?
2. Does technical change present business with an opportunity or a threat? Explain using examples.
3. 'The extent to which firms make use of information technology will inevitably determine their success in the future.' Discuss this view.

Data response question

Read the following article, which is reproduced from *The Sunday Times* of 16 September 2001. Then answer the questions that follow.

Wave energy

Britain's fading reputation as the pioneer of wave energy will be either overturned or confirmed by the development of a new offshore generating plant. Developed by Wavegen, an Inverness-based company, the floating platform aims to produce enough electricity to power 1400 Scottish island homes.

The £5 million device translates the up and down motion of the waves into energy to drive a turbine. Anchored to the seabed four miles off the coast of Orkney, it will route electricity to the island by submarine cable.

Project X is being developed behind closed doors while patents are sought. The move out to sea represents a brave gamble by Wavegen, which until now has harnessed natural wave energy only on or near coastlines.

The benefits of moving offshore to harness the ocean's energy are huge, according to industry experts. 'If we could fully utilize the offshore resource, we could run the whole of the UK's electricity demand for 40 per cent of the time in winter months,' says Professor Stephen Salter, of Edinburgh University's wave power group.

If successful, the floating platform could re-establish Britain as the world leader in wave technology. The Hawaiians, among others, have already shown an interest in the development.

Wavegen has a number of obstacles to overcome if it is to make a commercial success of Project X. For a start the cost of operating and maintaining a generator offshore is roughly double that of one on the coastline. 'It is a complicated design problem. You have to do something to dodge the really big waves. It's an uncertainty investors are very worried about,' said Salter.

1. What are the likely future benefits of developing wave power?
   [3 marks]
2. Who would be likely to fund the development of an offshore generating plant, and why? [3 marks]
3. Why would it be important to get patents for a new invention of this kind? [3 marks]
4. Why is the project risky? [3 marks]
5. Evaluate the advantages and disadvantages of this project. Outline the circumstances in which going ahead would turn out to be a good decision. [8 marks]

Chapter Six

Social and cultural influences

'True genius resides in the capacity for the evaluation of uncertain, hazardous and conflicting evidence.'
Sir Winston Churchill

Social and cultural influences are very diverse, including a wide range of different factors, many of them unrelated to one another. Some have an impact on the way businesses market their products. Others may affect production, human resource management strategies and other aspects of business decision-making. They include:

● population changes

● trends which affect **social class**, including education

● **social attitudes**

● **cultural preferences** and health issues

● global culture variations

● changes in the structure of the labour market

● the impact of the **black** (or informal) **economy**.

Before examining these influences, we should consider PEST analysis. This is a systematic way of grouping and examining the external influences on the business. The letters stand for Political, Economic, Social and Technology. PEST analysis involves a review of the situation in which the business finds itself, which can be used to inform important decisions. It may be possible to avoid mistakes which could result from failing to gather all of the relevant information beforehand.

Political influences include government policies and the law, which are dealt with in Chapters 7 and 8. They also include those major events which force businesses to reassess their positions. Examples include the Asian financial crisis of 1997–99, wars and terrorism and significant oil price changes.

Economic influences are all those factors which are likely to affect the profitability of the business. The level of demand, the extent of the competition, the state of the business cycle and current economic policies may all be important. These appear in Chapters 2, 3, 4 and 7.

Social influences include changes in the population and its **age**

```
┌─────────────────────────────────────────────────────────────────┐
│                        Change in the UK                           │
│                                                                   │
│  ● Saga's turnover grew as the number of people over the age of 50│
│    increased. They provide a growing market for holidays and      │
│    financial products.                                            │
│                                                                   │
│  ● The NHS grew steadily as the demands of an ageing population   │
│    made themselves felt. Nursing homes, too, increased in number. │
│    The demand for drugs to treat arthritis is expected to increase│
│    dramatically.                                                  │
│                                                                   │
│  ● The number of Mothercare outlets shrank as fewer babies were   │
│    born.                                                          │
│                                                                   │
│  ● In the 1950s, parents used to pay for elocution lessons for    │
│    their children, so they could avoid developing regional        │
│    accents. As these accents became more acceptable, elocution    │
│    teachers more or less vanished.                                │
│                                                                   │
│  ● Sales of organic food grow as more people worry about the      │
│    chemicals used in conventional agriculture and their impact on │
│    people and wildlife.                                           │
│                                                                   │
│  ● Sales of ready-to-eat meals have increased as more women work  │
│    full-time and more men live alone.                             │
│                                                                   │
└─────────────────────────────────────────────────────────────────┘
```

structure, changes in lifestyles and the attitudes of society. Culture can greatly affect the way people respond to different marketing strategies. These influences will be examined later in this chapter.

Technology is important in that, over time, the optimum production strategies will change. To the extent that competing businesses are changing the technologies they use, there will be serious pressure to cut costs and perhaps also prices. These threats may be counterbalanced by the opportunities for new product development. These issues were addressed in Chapter 5.

Population changes

Demographic changes involve changes in the size and structure of the population. A growing population indicates potential for growing markets and also often a growing labour force. Of particular importance is the age structure of the population, which will change the relative size of various market segments.

Figure 18 shows how the EU population is expected to age. The impact on the size of age-related market segments may be considerable. Of course, birth rate projections can be wrong.

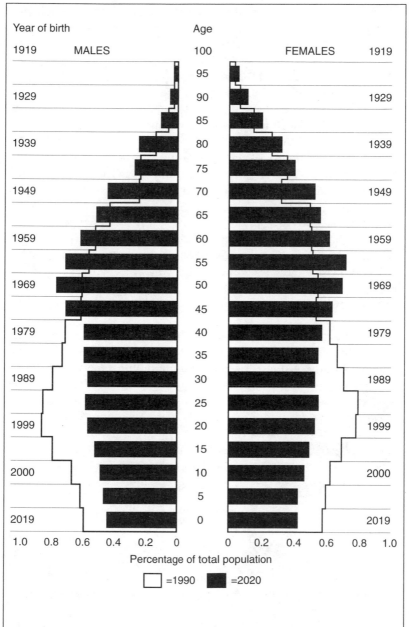

Figure 18 EU population pyramids, 1990 and the projection for 2020

Migration affects the total population, as well as the birth rate. Immigrants can be an important source of recruits to the labour force, because they tend to be of working age.

Changes in the social structure

Social structure can be defined in a range of ways. The British have always been accused of paying great attention to social class, and market research uses the standard divisions to help predict market trends. Figure 19 shows these.

Equally, the structure of the population can be defined by gender, location (rural versus urban or regional) and population density. These can all be important in identifying market segments, as can attitudes to environmental problems.

The UK is currently undergoing a significant change in social structure because more people are going to university. The government's target for this is 50 per cent. Many more people will in the future perceive themselves as being educated, whatever the level they have reached. Emphasis placed by the government on 'lifelong learning' is adding to the widespread sense of being capable of personal development.

The impact of this change is visible in the data on book and newspaper sales. A few years ago the demise of both products was predicted, on the grounds that everything would be online. Clearly,

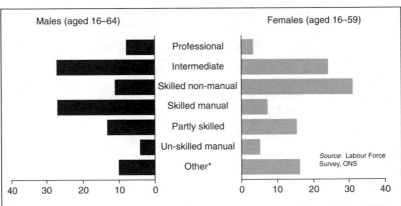

*Includes members of the armed forces, those who did not state their current or last occupation and those who had not worked in the last eight years.

Figure 19 The UK population of working age, by gender and social class, spring 2000 (percentages)

Table 7 National newspaper circulation trends, 1994–2000 (thousands)

	1994	2000	+ or – 94/00
Popular dailies			
The Sun	4078	3388	–16.9
Daily Mail	1775	2333	31.4
The Mirror	2494	2085	–16.4
The Express	1338	966	–27.8
Daily Star	744	552	–25.8
Popular dailies total	11 776	9912	–15.8
Quality dailies			
Daily Telegraph	1040	989	–4.9
The Times	542	676	24.7
The Guardian	401	357	–11.0
The Independent	281	201	–28.5
Financial Times	170	180	5.9
Quality dailies total	2438	2403	1.4
All national dailies	14 214	12 315	–13.4

Source: *Marketing Pocket Book 2002,* NTC Publications Ltd.

reading a book even on a laptop lacks cosiness and is uncomfortable in bed and there is no spine to look good on the shelves. (We know that more books are bought than are read.) In any event, Tables 7 and 8 show that the predictions were premature.

Table 8 Retail value of book sales in the UK (percentage change in real terms)

	Consumer	Academic/professional
1990–91	0.7	–1.6
1991–92	–0.5	5.1
1992–93	7.8	0.6
1993–94	2.3	1.2
1994–95	3.8	–1.7
1995–96	–6.7	–1.1
1996–97	4.0	1.3
1997–98	4.2	2.2
1998–99	3.0	–0.4

Excludes school books. Source: Publishers Association

Social and cultural attitudes

Culture means the **values**, beliefs and attitudes which are commonly held by a group of people. Society as a whole has certain cultural features. This culture will vary from one nation to another. Within any one society there will also be **sub-cultures**, groups of people with particular identifiable interests.

Understanding cultures is a vital element in the planning of many marketing campaigns. Mass markets are possible where the product is likely to appeal to a wide range of people. Market segments and niches will attract businesses which cater for the needs of individual sub-cultures. Business success is often determined by the extent to which producers understand their markets.

A new approach – mass customization – is allowing some manufacturers to produce the precise model that the customers want. They respond to the customer order, creating the product exactly as specified. This is happening with cars particularly, but also with refrigerators and washing machines, window frames and kitchens. It may spread to other products. It makes it easier for businesses to tailor the product to the needs of particular groups.

Social attitudes can have a significant impact on business. Sometimes the changes in attitude produce a change in tastes which simply shifts the pattern of demand. In the 1950s, most people either did not do much to improve their homes, or paid someone else to do it for them. Over the years, many people have felt an increasing urge to improve their homes by their own efforts. This created an opportunity for businesses which could offer DIY products, sometimes with advice about what to do with them.

Dolly the sheep

In 1997, scientists at the Roslin Institute in Scotland, an agricultural research centre, succeeded in cloning a sheep. The technical developments they pioneered have many possible applications in farming. But now, the institute says, the UK has become 'a hostile environment' for agricultural research.

Graham Bullfield, the director, says that companies are increasingly shifting their research to the US. That is in stark contrast to biomedical research, where an enlightened legal framework has made the UK the best place to do cloning and stem cell research which can be used to cure human disease. 'The institute could have played a significant role in developing safer and healthier foods', says Mr Bullfield, 'but the hostility to genetically modified food meant no one in the UK was interested in using biotechnology to overcome the problems of intensive farming.'

Other changes in social attitudes may affect some organizations in a very negative way.

Standards, health and safety

Generally, consumer expectations about safety standards and quality have risen over the years. Some of this change has been embodied in new laws. Other changes reflect the fact that more consumers complain about unacceptable product features. High standards of customer service are expected.

Sometimes social attitudes are changed by new information which becomes available. The realization that eating red meat may have an impact on the incidence of heart disease and other health problems has had major effects on the pattern of meat consumption. BSE disease accentuated these trends. Table 9 shows how patterns of meat eating have been affected.

Table 9 Animal sales in the UK

	1973	1989	1999
Cattle (thousands)	3294	3414	2217
Calves (thousands)	142	28	75
Sheep and lambs (thousands)	11759	19618	19116
Poultry (millions)	400	644	833

Source: ONS, *Annual Abstract of Statistics*, 1985 and 2001.

Cultural preferences

Meat sales have shown other evidence of cultural changes. Many people have become increasingly concerned about animal welfare. During the 1980s, there was a rising tide of concern about the way in which veal was produced. Protesters blockaded the channel ports to try to stop exports of calves to France, where the meat is popular. They drew attention to the unpleasant conditions under which many calves lived their short lives. Sales fell away and veal more or less vanished from the supermarket shelves. It is still to be found in some restaurants and farm shops. Table 9 shows how sales dropped.

Many businesses are sensitive to cultural preferences, being essentially market-oriented in their approach. However, businesses can be caught out by attitudinal changes which are not always predictable. Equally, they may benefit from a shift in tastes which is determined by external influences and leads to increased demand.

Global culture variations

There are often significant cultural differences between countries. Sometimes perceived differences are really just stereotypes. Nevertheless there are known differences in tastes and preferences and also in the ways in which businesses operate. It is important for businesses which export to be aware of these.

These differences in culture will help to determine whether the product will be competitive in the individual market. The Covent Garden Soup Company exports to France but it pays great attention to its distribution system so that the soup is really fresh when it goes on sale, despite the journey. If freshness could not be guaranteed, the discriminating French shopper would be quite uninterested.

Some help comes from the Department of Trade and Industry. It is part of its remit to advise businesses which want to export about the markets they are considering. Obviously, potential exporters of food and beverages need to be clear about eating and drinking habits in their anticipated markets. They need to do their market research at least as carefully they would in their domestic market.

Clothing, footwear and the fashion market in Japan

Outside of the EU, Japan is the second largest export market for clothing and accessories. As a result of increased foreign travel and exposure to international media, the Japanese have in recent years developed an appetite for western styles and designer labels.

Fashion for the younger generation, in particular, is responding to the need for individuality and identity – hence the strong market for streetwear and clubwear.

The spending power of women in their mid-20s to mid-30s is becoming increasingly important in the Japanese clothing industry. They are looking for competitively priced products, along with innovation and individuality, whilst maintaining high quality. UK suppliers are especially well positioned to meet the needs of this growing market.

Shoes, suits, blouses etc. are usually purchased in department stores, and many store chains, eager to attract new customers, are expanding their floor space and mixing products to appeal to the younger female market. Speciality stores are also popular purchasing sites for menswear and womenswear, followed by supermarkets and mail order.

Imports from the USA and Europe are now growing, with the UK gaining an increase in market share over the Italians (the second largest supplier of clothing to Japan after China). British apparel exports to Japan currently total around £232 million.

Source: DTI website

Some companies, like Coca Cola, can mount an advertising campaign covering most of the world, and it will work. Others leave most of the marketing to people located in individual markets, so that they can fit the advertizing to the characteristics and culture of that particular market. This holds irrespective of whether the product is an international brand.

Changes in the structure of the labour market

Labour markets have many individual cultural features and these do change over time:

● The willingness to acquire skills changes.

● The willingness to do unskilled work may be a significant factor, creating recruitment problems. For example, employment opportunities in farming in the Lake District are diminishing, but few of the people who leave farming want to do unskilled work in tourism.

● Attitudes to part-time work and to short-term contracts vary, unless lack of choice creates an imperative.

● In the past there has been a massive fall in **trade union** membership, which signals a trend towards more individual negotiation and less collective bargaining.

● **Flexibility** has increased. More people are prepared to undertake a range of tasks, given suitable training. It is usually accepted now that people will not necessarily pursue the same career or stay in the same job throughout their working lives.

Some of these changes reflect the way employers have moved in adopting innovative human resource management policies. But also, attitudes have changed in ways which make people more flexible about employers' requirements. An increase in the general level of education and training has helped – many people actually can do more than used to be the case.

The role of the trade unions

In 1980, 13 million people belonged to trade unions. By 1990 there were just under 10 million, and in 1995 there were 8 million. This fall reflected the fact that a great deal of union membership had been concentrated in the manufacturing industries which suffered most in the two recessions of 1981–82 and 1990–92. These industries did recover but they did it by investing in capital rather than re-employing their lost workers.

After that, the numbers sank more slowly, until 2000 when there was a small rise, brought about by the increase in employment. Still, union membership is more common among older employees, those with long service and employees in the public sector. Men are more likely to join a union than women.

The underlying culture of trade unions has meanwhile changed dramatically. It is a long time since confrontational tactics were widely seen to secure better pay. Secret ballots before industrial action have made strikes unusual. Where unions operate most effectively, they provide a mechanism for close communication with employers.

KEY WORDS

Social class

Social attitudes

Cultural preferences

Age structure

Demographic changes

Market segments

Social structure

Values

Sub-cultures

Trade unions

Flexibility

Further reading

Brooks, I., and Weatherston, J., Chapter 5 in *The Business Environment*, 2nd edn, FT/Prentice Hall, 2000.

Chambers, I., and Gray, D., Unit 20 in *Business Studies*, 2nd edn, Causeway Press, 2000.

Marcouse, I. *et al.*, Unit 84 in *Business Studies*, Hodder & Stoughton, 1999.

The Economist, Chapter 5 in *The Economist Guide to Economic Indicators*, 2000.

Useful websites

- The Department of Trade and Industry: www.dti.gov.uk.

• www.tradepartners.gov.uk provides details of various overseas markets which show how businesses need to assess national variations.

Essay topic

Using PEST analysis, identify the external influences on a business you have studied. Evaluate the importance of social and cultural influences on the decisions which this business has to make.

Data response question

Read the piece below concerning one company in the food-processing industry. Then answer the questions that follow.

... and chips

McCain, the Canadian frozen chip producers, are building a chip-making plant at Rugeley in Staffordshire which will take 6 per cent of the British potato crop. The cost will be £70 million. The chips will be destined for the catering trade. This will free up capacity in the two existing factories in Scarborough and Peterborough, which are to concentrate on the retail market.

Sales of frozen potato products have been growing at 5 per cent a year for thirty years. Nick Vermont, managing director of McCain GB, says the home-made chip is an anachronism. Demand for convenience foods is linked to falling skill levels in the catering industry and among individual consumers. Oven-ready chips and microwave chips have reduced consumption of mashed, boiled and roast potatoes.

The plant is to employ 150 at first, rising to 450 if the factory can expand. It will probably create another 1000 jobs in agriculture in the West Midlands area. This is good news for farmers who suffered from the effects of foot and mouth disease. 'The strength of the pound would have made the continent more attractive to some investors. But McCain is a private, family-owned business which takes the long-term view,' said Mr. Vermont.

1. Why is demand for frozen chips rising so strongly?   [4 marks]
2. To what extent are social and cultural changes important in McCain's decision?   [5 marks]
3. Explain why some investors might have preferred to invest in other parts of the EU.   [5 marks]
4. At the time of the investment decision, there was much talk of impending recession. McCain appear not to have been affected by this. Give three possible reasons for this.   [6 marks]

Chapter Seven

Legal influences

'The government has reformed the labour market to combine fairness and flexibility. We have introduced a set of minimum standards at the workplace, such as the minimum wage. These standards are about basic decency and are not an obstacle to running businesses successfully.'
The Labour Party's Business Manifesto, 2001

The legal influences on businesses are generally embodied in the laws passed by parliament. These laws then become subject to a body of **case law**. As infringements come to light, the alleged perpetrators are challenged in the courts. The decisions made by the courts create the case law and tell us how each law is actually being applied in practice.

In some areas of business law, much of the work is done by 'regulatory bodies'. The **Equal Opportunities Commission** may investigate cases of gender discrimination. The **Financial Services Authority** (FSA) supervises investment advisers, building societies and insurance companies, among many other businesses in the financial sector. The **Office of Fair Trading** (OFT) is responsible for the operation of consumer protection and competition law.

In addition to the law, there are also many regulations. These are not strictly speaking laws. Often they go into a level of detail which would not be found in acts of parliament. They may relate to product safety or standards or dispute resolution. **Regulations** can be laid down by quangos (quasi autonomous non-governmental organizations), such as Ofgem (the regulatory body for the energy industries). Some industry associations such as the **Advertising Standards Authority** (ASA) are known as self-regulatory organizations and lay down standards for the industry.

The privatized industries which are regarded as having potential monopoly powers all have regulatory bodies such as Oftel and Ofwat.

Regulation can itself become a source of monopoly power. When this has been seen to happen in the past, industries such as the buses and the banks have been **deregulated**; i.e. subjected to much lighter controls.

New laws and regulations may reflect quite strong democratic pressures. The difficulty of getting planning permission can be a problem for some businesses which want to expand, but can be important in protecting the environment in ways that many people actually want.

Consumer protection

Some of the legal constraints on business are framed in the interests of the consumer. The objective is to prevent consumers from being exploited by businesses which act in unethical ways. The implementation of consumer protection law is in the hands of the Office of Fair Trading.

- The Sale of Goods Act 1979 specifies that all products be 'of merchantable quality', so that they are suitable for their purpose. This is a wide-ranging requirement and the retailer is responsible for ensuring that it happens. This makes it easy for people to complain if necessary.

- The Trade Descriptions Act 1968 requires that products are what they say they are and that no misleading claims are made.

- The Food Safety Act 1990 covers everyone who produces or sells food products and lays down many strict rules about the production and handling of food.

- Weights and measures legislation sets up tough enforcement provisions to ensure that traders of all kinds give full measure when they are selling.

A consumer problem

A recent problem the OFT has resolved was concerned with fitted kitchens and bathrooms, where the problem was with full payment in advance. To buy a fitted kitchen/bathroom, the consumer has to pay up front because it is difficult for suppliers if they fit the kitchen/bathroom and then the consumer cannot pay.

However, this means that if the supplier does an unsatisfactory job, it can be hard for the consumer to get redress. In essence, the OFT felt what was needed was an honest broker. A solution was agreed with two of the largest suppliers, MFI and B&Q, which involves an independent trade body, Qualitas, providing a dispute resolution service. Qualitas holds back 20 per cent of payment until the dispute is resolved. This sensible commercial arrangement rectifies an imbalance that was causing quite a lot of consumer detriment judging by complaints received by the Office.

Source: 'Economic policy for competition and consumers', John Vickers, Director General of Fair Trading, in *Teaching Business and Economics*, summer 2001

The OFT can investigate any instances where unfair trading practices are suspected and can prosecute if that is appropriate. However, the existence of a body which energetically pursues the consumer interest makes infringements fairly infrequent. Businesses usually observe the way that the law works and try to keep within it.

From the point of view of the business, consumer protection will sometimes lead to increased costs of production. However, to the extent that it leads to products being better value for money, this is not necessarily a bad thing. The law puts all producers on a level playing field.

Competition law

The first anti-monopoly law in the UK was passed in 1948. Since then, a succession of laws has defined **anti-competitive practices** much more carefully and greatly increased the impact on certain kinds of business behaviour. Areas of concern include mergers and restrictive practices. The latter are simply strategies to reduce and restrict the effects of competition on the business.

The most important laws are outlined below.

- The Restrictive Practices Act 1956 set up the Restrictive Practices Court and required businesses to register any agreements which effectively restricted trade. Subsequent Restrictive Practices Acts in 1968 and 1976 had a strengthening effect.

- The Fair Trading Act 1973 defined a legal monopoly as a business with a 25 per cent market share and created the OFT and the post of Director General of Fair Trading, strengthening competition law considerably. It laid down the rules for referring mergers to the **Competition Commission** and provides for some monopolies to be investigated if there is cause for concern.

- The Competition Act 1980 defined anti-competitive practices more clearly and made it possible for them to be investigated first by the OFT and then by the Competition Commission. Businesses can complain about rival firms to the OFT and get the complaint investigated. If the offending company will not submit to voluntary undertakings, the complaint goes to the Competition Commission, which will investigate and report in greater depth.

- The Competition Act 1998 further strengthened the legislation by bringing it more closely into line with EU practice. It gives the OFT greater powers to investigate (including dawn raids). It makes it an offence for a business to 'abuse a dominant position', and the OFT can impose fines of up to 10 per cent of turnover in the UK.

Anti-competitive practices

The terms 'restrictive' or 'anti-competitive' practice are applied to any agreement to fix prices, restrict output, divide up the market, set up exclusive dealerships or discriminate between customers. A group of businesses that make an agreement of this sort is called a cartel. For a long time, the car dealers managed to preserve exclusive rights backed by the car manufacturers. However, this is now coming to an end as a result of action by the EU competition authorities.

Several recent cases have demonstrated that the 1998 legislation has made a real difference to competition policy. In late 2001, the government proposed to give the OFT sweeping new powers. The people responsible for creating cartels would receive prison sentences. Some business leaders are opposed to this.

John Cridland, deputy director general of the Confederation of British Industry said: '... premature criminalization will put UK companies at a competitive disadvantage to rivals in the EU. The proposals could backfire, causing companies to clam up on the provision of information.' It is clear that the evidence which would be gathered by the Competition Commission in a criminal case would have to be stronger than it is in the investigations carried out under the existing law. The whole system would become more like that of US competition policies.

CD prices have been investigated, as well as DVD prices, by the OFT.

Dawn raids

Late in 2001, the OFT raided the offices of Nike and JJB sports, among other sports retailers. It did this without warning, and took away quantities of papers for study. The OFT said: 'No assumption should be made at this stage that there has been an infringement of the law. We will not be in a position to decide that until we have all the facts.'

Fans have felt for a long time that the prices for replica kit are very high. A new shirt can cost more than £40. The OFT has investigated before. In 1999, the Football Association, the Premier League and the Scottish Football Association undertook to take action to ensure that manufacturers and retailers would not try to fix retail prices. Many football clubs sell replica kit in their shops and on their websites.

JJB Sports, one of the largest sportswear retailers, said after the raid that it had never been involved in price-fixing.

Find out from the OFT website what the outcome was and consider the resulting impact.

Mergers

The Competition Commission has changed its name several times over the years but the essentials remain the same. It has an important role in investigating possible mergers as well as existing monopolies. The basic objective is to prevent business behaviour which is against the public interest. If the commission finds that there is, or is likely to be, a monopoly, or an abuse of monopoly power, it will make recommendations to the OFT and the Secretary of State that action be taken.

Where mergers involve multinationals, they may be dealt with under EU regulations. The European Community Merger Regulation (ECMR) can even take a position on mergers between US companies if they are likely to affect markets in the EU. The merger of Boeing and McDonnell Douglas in 1997 brought about a sharp exchange of views before it went ahead.

Employment law

The scope and complexity of employment legislation has been greatly increased in recent years. Many of its provisions emanate from the EU, especially since the advent of the single market. This involves creating a level playing field for all the businesses wherever they are in the EU. So it follows naturally that they must all be subject to the same obligations to their employees.

Employment law covers:

- the **minimum wage**
- **health and safety**
- redundancy payments
- equal opportunities
- trade unions
- unfair dismissal
- **employee involvement** requirements
- the working time directive
- parental leave.

Many employment regulations do increase costs of production. However, some businesses want to behave responsibly towards their employees anyway, and the law requires all to do the same. With a level playing field, competition is likely to be fairer. (This issue will reappear in Chapter 10.) The question of the overall impact on business of regulation in total will be addressed in Chapter 8.

The Employment Relations Directorate of the Department of Trade and Industry (DTI) deals with many aspects of employment legislation. It covers both individual rights and collective rights. As well as helping to improve employer understanding of the law, it tries to encourage greater flexibility in the labour market.

Minimum wage legislation

The minimum wage for 2001/2002 was set at £4.10 an hour, or £3.50 for the age group 18–21. When the minimum wage was first introduced, there was some concern that because it would raise the cost of employing people, it might deter employers from taking on some labour. It could have reduced the level of employment.

Research has shown that in fact the minimum wage has had little if any effect on employment. Employers have accepted it. This may be because it is actually quite low, although its impact varies very much from one region to another. It has had little impact of any kind in London and the South East because wage rates there are typically well above the minimum. In the North East and north Wales, for example, where wages are considerably lower, the minimum wage has had a more significant impact.

Health and safety

Health and safety regulations have been in place for some time but they have been greatly strengthened by the EU. They are decided by majority voting, so once the regulations are agreed on that basis they apply to all.

The Health and Safety at Work Act 1974 gives all employers a duty to ensure that the workplace is physically safe. It also requires that there be training and supervision which is adequate to prevent accidents. Recognized trade unions can appoint safety representatives who can investigate problems and liaise with safety inspectors and the management. The enforcement of health and safety regulations rests with the Health and Safety Executive (HSE).

Redundancy

Where employees are unavoidably made redundant, they may qualify for redundancy payments. They have to have been working for the employer for more than two years. Redundancy pay is calculated as:

- for 18–21 year olds, half a week's pay for each year of service
- for 22–40 year olds, one week's pay for each year of service
- for 41–65 year olds, one and a half week's pay for each year of service.

This does give employees of long standing some protection. It also makes employers careful when recruiting employees to take on no more than they really need. They may give short-term contracts as a result. This can make for a feeling of insecurity. For people made redundant after a long period of employment, the money can provide the funds to set up a new business, perhaps one which will satisfy a growing demand.

Equal opportunities law

Since the Equal Pay Act was passed in 1970, employers have been required to offer men and women equal pay for equal work.

This was followed up by the Sex Discrimination Act 1975, which defined and prohibited a number of practices used in recruitment, promotion, dismissal and the provision of benefits. The Equal Opportunities Commission (EOC) was set up to monitor and enforce the law.

The Race Relations Act 1976 outlawed racial discrimination in both hiring and promotion. It set up the Commission for Racial Equality to keep the law under review and recommend change when necessary.

The Disability Discrimination Act 1995 requires employers to treat disabled people in the same way that they would others. They must also make provision for disabled access where appropriate, so that it is actually practical for them to employ some disabled people.

All of the equal opportunities legislation has had some effect on discrimination in the labour market, but in none of these areas does true equality of opportunity yet exist. It has been found that some employers which do have an equal opportunities policy have still not actually changed their customary practices enough to promote equality actively. 'Institutionalized racism' is a term devised to cover the situation where there is theoretical racial equality, but discrimination continues to occur. This can happen where not all the people who are working in an organization are fully committed to the policy.

Real or imaginary equality?

Irene McClure, policy officer at the Commission for Racial Equality, has found that workplace equality is far from guaranteed in many companies. 'It is no longer enough for candidates who want to ensure fair treatment at work to ask at interview whether an employer has a policy. They will need to explore exactly what it consists of.'

'The law lays down basic standards, but to translate these into action, a company must have specific policies', says Dianah Worman, adviser on equal opportunities at the Chartered Institute of Personnel and Development. 'Furthermore, the company must ensure policies are understood and adhered to by all employees.'

Littlewoods is one company that has made a big effort to renovate its policy. Since the 1960s it has been running programmes to boost the representation of ethnic minority employees and promote opportunities for women. As early as 1970, paternity leave was introduced. In 1994 a review was carried out by the EOC. This made 44 recommendations to integrate the policies, and action on them, into the core functions of the business. Among the improvements made since at Littlewoods are a complete overhaul of the remuneration package, improvements to employee communications, and management development to support culture change.

Independent on Sunday, 22 October 2000

Trade union legislation

Over the past twenty years, changes in the law affecting trade unions has actually reduced the constraints on business. The five Employment Acts passed between 1980 and 1990 made industrial action more difficult and this greatly reduced trade union pressure on employers. The most important provisions were:

- giving employers the right to sue trade unions for loss of earnings
- allowing pickets only in the employees' own place of work
- allowing strikers to be dismissed under certain circumstances
- requiring secret ballots before a strike
- changing the rules concerning union recognition, so that there is much less obligation on the employer to negotiate with trade unions.

These laws were enacted at a time when many businesses were making people redundant. These people then sought alternative work and competitive pressures in the labour market became much greater. This made it easier for employers to recruit, except for those skills which continued to be in short supply.

The Employment Relations Act 1999

This Act embodied a number of regulations which related to the adoption of the Social Chapter of the Maastricht Treaty of the EU, signed in 1991. At that time, the UK government opted out of the Social Chapter because so many influential business people objected to its provisions. The new Labour government opted in immediately after the 1997 election victory. The Act followed this up with the necessary legislation to harmonize employment law with the rest of the EU. The provisions included:

- new rules relating to unfair dismissal
- the working time directive
- employee involvement
- parental leave regulations.

Unfair dismissal

If an employee has been employed for more than one year, and if the person feels he or she has been dismissed unfairly, then that individual can appeal to an employment tribunal. The reasons might be because the employee was trying to get full rights under existing employment law while the employer was trying to get out of the full obligations. For example, an employee who was sacked for asking to be paid the minimum wage would have a good case for compensation.

Unfair dismissal does not apply when a fixed-term contract has come to an end, or when the employee has been dismissed for valid disciplinary reasons or when there are genuine redundancies.

The working time directive

Over a 17-week period, employees may not work more than an average of 48 hours a week. However, they are allowed to opt out voluntarily, so this provision does not often impinge heavily on employers. Four weeks' paid leave is required. There are requirements about rest breaks and also night work.

Employee involvement requirements

One of the big sticking points for UK businesses when faced with the Social Chapter was the employee involvement. They have tended to lag far behind similar businesses in the rest of the EU. Although they have for many years had to consult employees when mass redundancies were contemplated, they have found ways to make sure this did not become onerous.

In fact, the intentions of the directive announced in 2001 are to improve communications rather than to prevent management from taking decisions. The penalties for non-compliance are not known at the time of writing, but it is clear that businesses will have to consult when corporate restructuring is planned and when benefits and rights may be changed.

The European Works Council directive applies to all multinational businesses with operations in two or more EU countries. They have works councils which consist of employee representatives from their organizations in each EU country. They can discuss common concerns such as job security and health and safety. Newspaper reports over several years suggest that businesses with experience of these consultations find them helpful rather than otherwise. In general, employee involvement has turned out to be much less frightening to UK businesses than they anticipated.

Parental leave
Statutory parental leave now consists of a total of thirteen weeks per child taken any time in the first five years of the child's life, for both parents. They must have been with the employer for a minimum of one year. Parents must be allowed to return to the same job after their leave, or at least something similar.

The next chapter reviews the overall impact of the regulatory framework on businesses.

KEY WORDS

Case law	Deregulation
Equal Opportunities	Anti-competitive practices
Commission	Mergers
Financial Services Authority	Competition Commission
Office of Fair Trading	Cartel
Regulation	Minimum wage
Advertising Standards	Health and safety
Authority	Employee involvement

Further reading

Chambers, I., and Gray, D., Units 80 and 81 in *Business Studies*, 2nd edn, Causeway Press, 2000

Dransfield, R., Chapters 7 and 8 in *Human Resource Management*, Heinemann Educational, 2000.

Gillespie, A., Chapter 3 in *Competitive Environment and External Influences*, Hodder & Stoughton, 2000.

Jewell, B., Chapter 8 in *An Integrated Approach to Business Studies*, 4th edn, Longman, 2000.

Useful websites

- The Food Standards Agency at www.foodstandards.gov.uk will give a good idea of what regulations look like in practice. Look at the food premises inspection programme.

- The Employment Relations Directorate: www.dti.gov.uk/er.

- The Office of Fair trading: www.oft.gov.uk.

Essay topics

1. Outline the likely effects of recent changes in employment legislation. To what extent can businesses expect to (a) gain and (b) lose?

2. Examine the outcome of a recent referral of a merger to the Competition Commission. What impact did this have on (a) the business and (b) the industry?

Data response question

The article below is taken from 'Economic policy for competition and consumers, by John Vickers, Director General of Fair Trading (*Teaching Economics and Business*, The Journal of the Economics and Business Education Association, summer 2001). Read the article and then answer the questions that follow.

Interbrew and Bass

The beer market has a small number of major brewers and wholesalers and has a history of government intervention. Vertical integration used to be the major competition concern as the large brewers with their pub estates were able to dampen competition from smaller rivals. Following a monopoly reference case in the late 1980s, the national brewers disposed of thousands of pubs and some brewers exited brewing altogether. The main competition concerns now appear to lie in increasing concentration in brewing and on-trade distribution.

In May 2000, the Belgian brewer Interbrew acquired the brewing interests of Whitbread. Since most of Whitbread's sales consisted of Interbrew's Stella Artois brewed under licence, this merger did not raise significant competition concerns and was cleared.

In June 2000, Interbrew announced its intention to acquire the brewing interests of Bass, which it did in August 2000 for £2.3 billion. The merger was initially an ECMR case, but because the competition concerns were mainly in the UK market, it was referred back to the UK.

The merger gave Interbrew market shares of 38 per cent of brewing and 33 per cent of on-trade wholesaling. Interbrew and Scottish and Newcastle would together have about 60 per cent of the industry, along with strong portfolios of leading brands.

In brewing, economies of scale in production and marketing are important and mean that entering the market on an efficient scale incurs large sunk fixed costs that cannot be recovered upon exit. Wholesale and distribution also has large sunk fixed costs and economies of scale are again very important. Many smaller brewers are thus reliant on larger brewers for access to retailers because it is not cost-effective for them to make small deliveries by other means. The large brewers can control access to parts of the market and can discriminate against brands that compete directly with their leading brands, resulting in higher prices and less choice.

In January 2001, the Competition Commission found this merger to be against the public interest. The Secretary of State's decision was that Interbrew should divest itself of the brewing interests of Bass Brewers.

[Postscript: Upon judicial review, Interbrew was ordered to sell its Carling, Caffrey's and Worthington brands. It was allowed to keep Tennent's, Bass Ale and Boddingtons brands, and some smaller breweries.]

1. Why do governments legislate to promote competition? [3 marks]
2. What advantages do big brewers have over smaller ones? [3 marks]
3. Why is the industry likely to involve some barriers to competition?
   [4 marks]
4. What problems did Interbrew have as a result of its takeover of Bass being referred to the Competition Commission?   [4 marks]
5. To what extent was the takeover of Bass by Interbrew likely to be against the public interest, on the evidence available at the time?
   [6 marks]

Chapter Eight

Political influences

'If any ask me what a free government is, I answer that for any
practical purpose, it is what the people think so.'
Edmund Burke, 1729–1797

Many people who work in business do have a view about the scale of
political influence on the business environment. It is extraordinarily
common to read reports or hear business people saying that the
government should interfere less.

In order to understand political influences on business it is really
necessary to ponder the past. This is all about how we got where we are
today. One of the most acute observers of business was the economist
Adam Smith, whose book *The Wealth of Nations*, published in 1776,
had a major impact on thinking in this area. He believed that it was the
economic freedom of individuals to set up in businesses which would
be profitable, which led to people's needs being met efficiently. His
views have been used to support the idea that government interference
makes life more difficult for businesses. Supporters of a 'laissez-faire'
approach to government believe that competition will be sufficient to
ensure that an economy prospers, without too much government
intervention.

After 1989

In 1989, the government of the USSR (Russia and the neighbouring
republics) decided that it would no longer use its defence forces to support
communist governments there and in eastern Europe. Up to that time, all
production and distribution decisions were made by government agencies
or branches of the communist party. Quite quickly these collapsed.
Private enterprise became possible.

Many of the state-owned factories had to close because they were too
inefficient to compete with imports. Private enterprises sprang up. But life
was difficult for them. There were very few controls on them, so fraud was
an ever-present threat as well as an opportunity. Valuable resources were
sold but the proceeds did not necessarily go to the rightful owner. On
average, incomes fell by 6.1 per cent a year in Russia, for the whole of the
1990s. Lack of clearly established property rights made it hard to plan
profit-making enterprises.

A laissez-faire system is *not* one without laws. The law of contract, which makes it possible for businesses to require payment from their customers, and weights and measures law, are two very basic and ancient examples of laws which facilitate trade. We take them for granted – but without them, running a business can be very difficult.

'Laissez faire' or intervention?

After about 1815, UK governments pursued the free market model and intervened very little. But then problems began to emerge. In 1848, the government passed the first Public Health Act – because unsanitary drains were leading to outbreaks of cholera. Then it became necessary to think of providing education because employers needed people who could read. And it became clear that left to themselves, businesses would try to form cartels and other monopolistic arrangements.

Intervention gradually increased. In 1945 it took a dramatic leap as the Labour government set up the National Health Service and nationalized the coal, rail, telephone and several other industries. These measures greatly increased the size of the public sector – that part of the economy owned or run by central or local government. The UK became a **mixed economy** with both public and private enterprises.

More dramatic change came in the 1980s, when privatization returned most of the nationalized industries to the private sector. This meant selling their shares to the general public. Those which had a monopoly in their market were given regulators such as Ofgem. You have already met regulation in many of its forms in Chapter 7. In theory, with privatized industries we get private-sector efficiency with regulation to protect the consumer.

Figure 20 shows that productivity (and therefore efficiency) did rise for the main privatized industries in the relevant time period. (Some of the improvement occurred before privatization, as the industries were encouraged to become more commercial.)

The EU, the single market and harmonization

Running parallel with UK government policy has been the influence of the European Union. The UK joined the EU in 1973. Even before this, UK trade with EU member countries was growing. The whole focus of UK trade shifted away from the US and the Commonwealth, towards the EU. Expanding markets in Europe became very important to many UK businesses. Figure 21 shows the current trade pattern.

An important element in the objectives of the EU is to have a single set of rules and regulations, which everyone must abide by. This is the so-called 'level playing field', meaning **harmonization**. So all across the

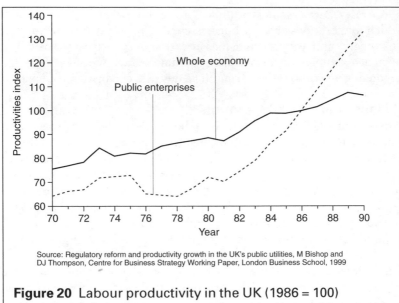

Source: Regulatory reform and productivity growth in the UK's public utilities, M Bishop and DJ Thompson, Centre for Business Strategy Working Paper, London Business School, 1999

Figure 20 Labour productivity in the UK (1986 = 100)

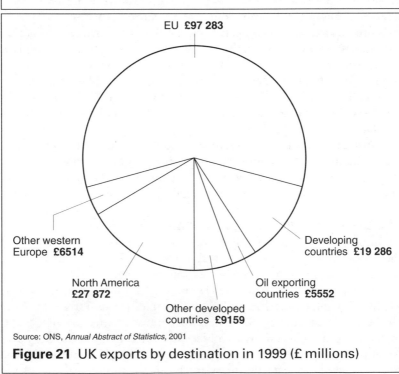

Source: ONS, *Annual Abstract of Statistics*, 2001

Figure 21 UK exports by destination in 1999 (£ millions)

EU, laws are closely aligned with one another. This encourages competition because all businesses have to produce to uniform standards. They must also treat their employees equally fairly. The competition policies which keep them from forming cartels and raising prices will be the same for all too. The regulations which have been set up to achieve EU objectives were dealt with in Chapter 7.

Regulation on the scale we now have in the EU cannot really be consistent with a laissez-faire philosophy. On the other hand, governments no longer try to run industries. They found out that they were not very good at running them profitably. With privatization right across the EU, they stopped trying. There are a lot of arguments about the effects of privatization. It can be argued that the combination of privatization and competition policy has increased the extent to which markets work efficiently to meet consumers' needs. Rising standards of living suggest that this may be true.

Compliance

All three of the UK's main political parties say they want to cut the amount of red tape which afflicts businesses, especially small ones. Every business must know about the regulations that apply to it. Big businesses can have a **compliance** department, which specializes in knowing the regulations and working to find the best ways to comply. The manager or owner of a small business has to do this while doing a host of other tasks. People do complain about it and it can be very costly.

As well as competition law and labour law, there are all the regulations pertaining to product standards and environmental regulations. Planning law creates particular problems. Before it can expand, a business must get planning permission for its new plant and buildings. This can take a long time.

The current government has introduced the Regulatory Reform Act 2001 and set up the Regulatory Impact Unit. Some regulations have been scrapped. The trouble is that safety requirements and environmental protection require an ever-increasing number of controls in order to avoid newly identified dangers. Businesses don't like red tape but people don't like risks being taken.

The UK government

On the whole, left-of-centre governments tend to be more interventionist than the more right-wing governments. They may also be more likely to raise taxes. They may have bigger expenditure plans. There are easily identified examples of these generalizations.

> ## Bosses can be held liable for workers' behaviour
>
> Lindsay Thomas owns and runs a convenience store on a large housing estate. Her manager dismissed a part-time assistant. This woman claimed that she been discriminated against as a woman and took the case to an employment tribunal.
>
> Lindsay did not want to go before the tribunal and her nervousness began to make her feel ill. She believed her manager, who said that he had caught the employee taking home groceries which she had not paid for. But her solicitor told her that it would be extremely difficult to prove that there had been no discrimination.
>
> For a while she contemplated paying the applicant to avoid having to go to the tribunal. In the end she won her case but the experience is not one that she wants to repeat.
>
> The Advisory, Conciliation and Arbitration Service (ACAS) tries to settle disputes before they go to a tribunal. It says that an increasing number of discrimination cases is being brought against small business owners.

- The Labour government which followed the 1997 election quickly signed up to the EU's Social Chapter, from which the previous government had opted out. This entailed more employment laws.

- The Liberal Democrats in the UK have for some years said they would raise the standard rate of tax to pay for increased spending on education and healthcare.

- Conservative governments steadily cut the standard rate of income tax from 33 per cent in 1979 to 23 per cent in 1997.

However, life is not so simple as these examples suggest. The same Labour government became *less* interventionist when it gave the Bank of England a large degree of independence in setting interest rates. The Conservatives *increased* spending on the NHS, mindful of the needs of the ageing population. It is wise to look at the costs and benefits of each measure and assess it on its merits.

A good way to think about the size of the government is to look at the data on public spending as a percentage of the gross domestic product (GDP). This rises during recession because of falling tax receipts and rising unemployment benefits. But on balance, for the past thirty years it has hovered around 41 per cent, rising very gradually to perhaps a current average of 42 per cent. The colour of the government has made remarkably little difference.

Public spending in the UK is very average in comparison with other developed countries. It is proportionately smaller than in Germany or Scandinavia, where welfare payments tend to be rather more generous. Similarly, the French have more and better public services. The public sector is much smaller in the US, but much the same in Canada. The absence of public healthcare for all, and relatively low welfare benefits, make the US government budget proportionately modest.

Government spending and taxes

Figure 22 shows how the government's budget breaks down. Even with a relatively low level of unemployment in the year concerned, social security is always the biggest item by far.

From 1999 to 2001, the government spent less than it received in tax revenue. In other words, there was a surplus. This reflected low levels of unemployment and growing incomes which provided extra tax revenue. In 2002, extra spending was planned for health and education and unexpected increases in defence spending looked likely. Recession

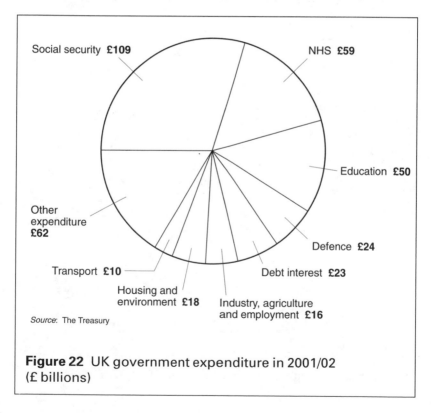

Figure 22 UK government expenditure in 2001/02 (£ billions)

was expected to lead to higher benefit payments and lower tax revenues.

Businesses are always very concerned about the rates at which **corporation tax** is levied. In 2001, the standard rate was 30 per cent of profits, with a special rate of 20 per cent for small businesses. The actual amount paid, though, depends heavily on investment allowances and other sources of relief. Actual amounts can be found in annual reports and accounts.

Figure 23 shows that corporation tax is not a big revenue raiser for the government. However, taken together, corporation tax, **business rates** (paid to local authorities) and employers' **national insurance** contributions are more significant.

Government sources of help

Businesses depend upon governments in a variety of ways.

● Regional policies provide some financial support to some businesses which are setting up in areas of high unemployment.

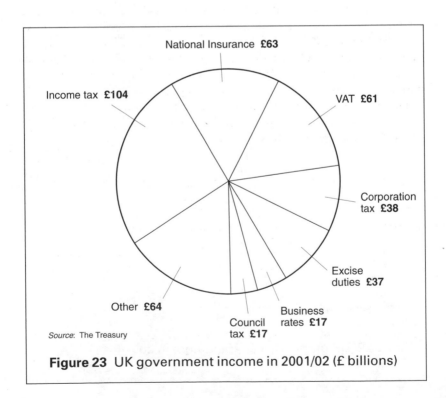

National Insurance **£63**

Income tax **£104**

VAT **£61**

Corporation tax **£38**

Excise duties **£37**

Other **£64**

Council tax **£17**

Business rates **£17**

Source: The Treasury

Figure 23 UK government income in 2001/02 (£ billions)

- Government support for research and development can benefit businesses with related interests. Of the funds for R&D, about 47 per cent comes from the UK private sector, about 32 per cent comes from the government, and the rest comes from charities or abroad. About one-third of the government share is devoted to defence – but even this can benefit private sector suppliers indirectly.

- The public sector is important to business as a provider of infrastructure – road and rail systems, public services and so on. However, in practice, transport plans have been subject to very long delays because they are always costly and involve playing off many different interest groups.

- For many businesses, the government is an important customer. For example, the NHS is a major customer for manufacturers of drugs and hospital equipment.

Collaboration with government

Businesses work with the government in some areas. The New Deal is a scheme to help unemployed 18–24 year olds who have been unemployed for six months or more to get training and find work. First they get intensive careers advice and help with job skills. After that if they are still unemployed they may get a subsidized job, voluntary work with training, or a place in full-time education. Employers work with government agencies to provide the necessary opportunities.

The National Institute for Economic and Social Research estimates that the New Deal has reduced youth long-term unemployment by 40 per cent. Employers may benefit from increased skill levels.

Transport 2010

'So Madam Speaker, these are new ideas, new powers, new resources and a new approach for a new century. It is on these foundations we are building today's ten-year programme. It is based on long-term investment by government and industry to modernize the country's transport system. It is vital for our economic success and the quality of our life, and it is excellent news for the manufacturers and the construction sector who will be able to plan for the long term.'

Source: excerpt from John Prescott's speech to the House of Commons on the Integrated Transport Plan, 27 July 2000

Political change and international trade

After 1989, many businesses thought that markets in the **transitional economies** of Russia and eastern Europe offered exciting possibilities. In some places this has happened. Poland, the Czech Republic and Hungary are doing well and are in the first wave of countries being considered for membership of the EU. Poland achieved an average growth rate during the 1990s of 4.7 per cent. Other countries, including Russia, have found the adjustment process so difficult that the market possibilities are quite limited.

Many Asian economies, making the transition from a low to a high level of economic development, have provided more promise for exporters. Even so, there have been some problems. 'The Asian Way' of doing business often involves helping business partners rather than applying hard commercial logic. Sometimes banks have continued to lend to businesses long after it is clear that they are not really profitable. Many Asian banks are burdened with bad debts, which will never be repaid. The governments of Japan and the Republic of Korea have grappled with this problem, which threatens the stability of their economies and of the surrounding region.

In this way, political problems can affect the export prospects of businesses far away on the other side of the world. There are numerous other political problems. Many UK businesses have interests in China. The Chinese government is still run by the communist party and the legal system there is still poorly equipped to deal with commercial disputes. The business environment is, at the very least, unpredictable. But China has 1.2 billion people, not all of whom are poor. As with some other transitional economies, it remains a potentially attractive market.

Barriers to trade

Many people worry about the impact of globalization. From the point of view of exporting businesses, global markets can be very profitable. Some businesses, of course, face competition from imports. The UK car and clothing industries, for example, are quite vulnerable.

Cheap imports mean cheap products for consumers. Sometimes paying less for what they want means that they can make their incomes go further – their standard of living rises. But jobs may be lost in domestic businesses which compete with imports.

People who work for exporters want export markets to grow. There could be more jobs. Pay may rise, to attract the extra labour. In fact, in any situation where trade patterns are changing, there are gainers and losers. If the losers are protected the gainers may not gain.

Table 10 Average annual per capita real income growth

	1980–90	1990–99
East Asia	8.8	9.1
Latin America and Caribbean	1.8	3.3
Middle East and North Africa	2.1	3.5
South Asia	5.7	5.6
Sub-Saharan Africa	2.0	2.2
Central Europe	1.8	3.0
Eastern Europe and Central Asia	3.9	-3.7
Industrialized countries	3.2	2.4

Source: International Economic Data Bank, Australian National University.

The **World Trade Organization** (WTO) was set up to make trade easier. It works to reduce import duties and ensure that member countries compete on equal terms. Most of the world's nations are now members. Many of the newer ones want to be able to use the WTO's disputes settlement mechanism.

On the whole, opening up export markets has created a lot of jobs in both developed and developing countries. Economic growth rates, in Asia in particular, have been built upon growing exports. Table 10 shows how incomes have been growing in parts of the world. Higher incomes mean bigger markets for businesses everywhere.

Violent conflicts

Violence can have very varied effects on businesses. If you happen to be hit directly by terrorists, of course, you will be badly affected. Your insurance company may have a problem too. On the other hand, if you manufacture weapons or other defence equipment, the outcome may be excellent for business.

In poor countries there is no question – wars reduce standards of living to sometimes desperate levels. In richer countries, the extra government spending can increase job opportunities and for some businesses, profits. It will not, of course, help to build schools and hospitals.

> ## KEY WORDS
>
> | | |
> |---|---|
> | Nationalization | Business rates |
> | Mixed economy | National insurance |
> | Privatization | Transitional economies |
> | Harmonization | World Trade Organization |
> | Compliance | Violence |
> | Corporation tax | |

Further reading

Brooks, I., and Weatherston, J., Chapter 7 in *The Business Environment*, 2nd edn, FT/Prentice Hall, 2000.

Chambers, I., and Gray, D., Unit 6 in *Business Studies*, 2nd edn, Causeway Press, 2000.

Hill, B., *The European Union*, 4th edn, Heinemann Educational, 2001.

Worthington, I., and Britton, C., Chapter 3 in *The Business Environment*, 3rd edn, FT/Prentice Hall, 2000.

Useful websites

- Detail on transport plans: www.detr.gov.uk.

- The government's gateway site: www.ukonline.gov.uk.

- International data: www.worldbank.org/data.

Essay topics

1. To what extent should managers welcome change?
   [AQA, specimen question, 2000]
2. Examine four ways in which government intervention can be helpful to businesses. In each case, evaluate the effectiveness of the policy.

Data response question

Read the piece below about just one of the commercial consequences of a terrorist action. Then answer the questions that follow.

An essential escape

When terrorists flew planes into the World Trade Center in New York and the Pentagon in Washington, DC, widespread economic distress was predicted. People were understandably nervy about flying, for a while. Restaurant takings slumped and holidays were cancelled. What did people do? In the week following the attack, the US population went out to the video shop. Takings went up by 13 per cent. This despite the fact that for the year previously, there had been a 9 per cent drop in demand.

US homes with DVD players registered a 25 per cent increase in demand in the same week. Videoscan, the monitoring service, said that more than half the top-selling titles were for children. Willie Wonka and the Chocolate Factory did particularly well.

1. Give three other examples of political events or trends which (for good or ill) have had an impact on businesses. Explain what happened. [6 marks]
2. For each of your examples, explain how the businesses concerned might react to the change in the business environment. [7 marks]
3. What types of business are most likely to be vulnerable to political changes? Provide as many examples as you can. [7 marks]

Chapter Nine

The environment

'The pursuit of sustainable development is not an option ... it is nothing more or less than a necessity for economic survival.'
Sir Ian Vallance

Many human activities have an effect on the ecological environment. Unfortunately, rising standards of living tend to increase this effect. Concern has been growing since the 1960s. Some improvements have been achieved. But as we learn more about the likely consequences of environmental degradation, anxiety has tended to increase.

Sustainable development

Environmentalists point out that we should not be using natural resources faster than they can be replaced. If we do, we are leaving for future generations an impoverished world. Few would disagree with this.

However, **sustainable development**, which avoids destroying resources, will happen only if we set about making improvements. New technologies have much potential. But sustainable production is often more costly than the existing production methods, so there are awkward, detailed issues which have to be debated both within businesses and in society as a whole.

The broad areas of environmental concern are numerous. They tend to centre on the types of air **pollution** which are likely to be connected to **climate change**. But there are many other issues:

- using depletable resources faster than they can be replaced – as with tropical hardwoods

- production processes which leak or discharge hazardous gases or materials into the atmosphere or water

- traffic **congestion**

- waste disposal

- reductions in biodiversity

- threats to the natural world from genetically modified (GM) foods.

External costs

Mostly, business costs are added up and captured in the profit and loss account. Wages, rents, raw material and capital equipment costs will all be there. But sometimes there is a hidden cost. It could come from pollution created during production, or from contamination of surrounding land by hazardous waste, or congestion created by deliveries in and out of the factory. There are many other examples.

These costs are known as **external costs**, because they are borne by third parties. People who have nothing to do with either the production or the use of the product experience a cost. This reduces their quality of life or perhaps actually costs them money. Breathing polluted air and getting asthma is unpleasant; sitting in a traffic jam may waste money. Sometimes external costs are described as **negative externalities**.

To deal with external costs, we can use the 'polluter pays' principle. This shifts the external cost on to the producer, and perhaps also the consumer. Various strategies are used, often government regulation or taxes.

Table 11 identifies the main polluters in the UK. The 'Other' category includes most business sources other than road transport and electricity supply, and government sources. The case study 'Unilever and freezers' shows how one problem product is being handled.

Table 11 Air pollutants by source in the UK in 1998 (percentages)

	Carbon dioxide	Carbon monoxide	Sulphur dioxide	Nitrogen oxides compounds	Volatile organic	Particulates
Road transport	21	73	1	46	27	24
Electricity supply	27	2	66	21	–	14
Domestic	16	5	3	4	2	16
Other	36	20	29	30	71	45
All sources (million tonnes)	148.5	4.8	1.6	1.8	2.0	0.2

Source: ONS, *Social Trends*, 2001.

Unilever and freezers

Our ice cream business provides thousands of freezers in shops around the world. Freezer technology is developing fast in response to concerns about climate change and ozone depletion. Early replacements for CFCs – gases called HFCs – are ozone-benign but have a high global warming potential. These gases – as well as others – are used as refrigerants and to produce the insulation used in cabinets.

Making a commitment to a particular freezer technology must be weighed up carefully because freezer cabinets have a long life. We therefore prefer to progress steadily with the adoption of any new approach and are determined to remain open to all emerging technologies.

Technology that uses hydrocarbons may be the best environmental option at present, but other new and emerging technologies could provide even better solutions in the future. Unilever wishes to remain in a position to review its choice of freezer technology and to adopt the best systems as they become available.

We do not consider that HFCs provide the right long-term solution. The insulation in cabinets we buy are foamed using hydrocarbons in countries where this is legally and practically possible. We are working together with our suppliers to find alternative refrigerants, and by 2005 our new cabinets will be HFC-free, assuming that this is commercially feasible and is allowed under local laws.

Source: Unilever website

The public response

People vary as to how much they worry about the environment. Some perceive the problems as being rather far away. They are preoccupied with survival right now, and it is hard to get them interested in the possibility that their children and grandchildren may have big problems.

Other people are very worried indeed. They feel that we are threatening the planet with greenhouse gases and unsustainable development. The greenhouse gases consist mainly of carbon dioxide, which comes from burning fossil fuels like oil. Many scientists now believe that they are causing global warming.

Emotions on these issues run high. The rest of this chapter will try to remove some of the heat from the debate and shed a little light instead. Facts are not always what they seem.

'The public' mostly fall into three categories:

RSPB: a pressure group

The Royal Society for the Protection of Birds has over a million members. It is a big enough organization to buy land for nature reserves. In the year 2000/01, it spent £3.5 million on new nature reserves and extensions to existing ones. It spent a further £9 million managing those reserves. It is able to buy whole farms and use them to experiment with farming techniques which may be 'bird-friendly'. Its annual budget is over £50 million and it spends just over £8 million of that on fundraising and administration. It has had some notable successes in encouraging rare species to breed. As a pressure group it may be able to encourage a general shift towards farming methods which preserve wildlife.

- the unworried
- the passionately concerned
- the large group in the middle who are concerned and want to see action, but not at any price and on everything.

Large numbers of the second two groups have joined **pressure groups**, set up to act and to lobby politicians. Pressure groups keep their members up to date, represent them at meetings with politicians, create a presence in the media, and generally campaign for their objectives. Many are small but some, like Friends of the Earth, are big organizations.

Marketing issues

The environmental lobby can be important in marketing terms. There is no doubt that some businesses use claims about environmental friendliness as part of their marketing pitch. However, this leaves us wondering whether the product really is as environmentally friendly as it claims to be, or whether the advertising is technically true but only a small part of the total picture. Equally, it is hard to tell whether the business is really acting responsibly, or just making the most of an advertising opportunity.

Pressure put on McDonald's led them to make more of their packaging bio-degradable. But many people still think that McDonald's activities are on the whole not good for the planet. How do we decide where the balance lies?

Until you read the case study on Unilever and freezers, you may not have realized that, although banning CFCs helped to protect the ozone layer, the substitute material creates greenhouse gases. We will return to the whole question of openness when we examine the progress made with audits.

Action by the government

Over the years, government action has made some difference to air and water quality. The clean air acts of the 1950s stopped people from burning coal and greatly reduced the amount of smoke in city atmospheres. Fish are returning to the Thames, it is said.

There are three important lines of attack for governments.

- Regulation limits the amount of pollutants which can be released into the atmosphere and rivers and on to land.

- Tradable permits allow maximum levels of emissions. If the business concerned cleans up its processes, it can sell its permit to another business. Over time the total level of pollution permitted can be reduced by selling fewer permits.

- Products which pollute can be taxed. The most newsworthy such tax is that on petrol and diesel for vehicles. The climate change levy is an interesting development too.

Regulation has to be enforced. Research done at the Harvard Business School found that 65 per cent of the Fortune 500 companies had at some time been charged with ethical crimes, many of which concerned **hazardous wastes**. Catching the offenders involves having enough inspectors with powers sufficient to enable them to investigate. This is harder than it might seem.

Tradable permits have to be enforced too. Perhaps most importantly, all of these measures, if successful, will tend to increase product prices to customers. This is where the crunch comes. How much will people pay to avoid environmental threats?

Petrol taxes

In an attempt to discourage vehicle use, the UK government introduced the fuel tax escalator in 1995. There were good reasons for this, besides meeting international obligations to reduce greenhouse gas emissions. Roads were becoming increasingly congested and delays were raising costs for many businesses.

Petrol had always been taxed but this allowed for increases of 6 per cent above the rate of inflation. Over a period of years, this had a considerable effect on fuel users. When Labour took over from the Conservatives in 1997, they continued the policy. By 2000, a strange coalition of individuals, hauliers and farmers had begun to protest so

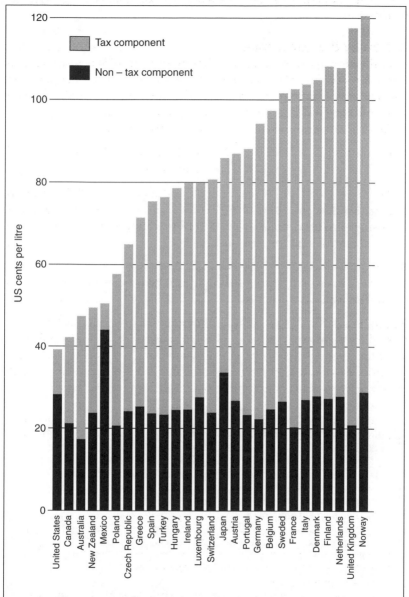

Figure 24 International prices and taxes for unleaded petrol in the third quarter of 1999

Source: Institute of Public Affairs

vigorously that the government decided to abandon the escalator. There were similar protests in other EU countries. Meanwhile, the US government had made a definite decision not to increase fuel taxes.

It is possible that technological developments will greatly reduce the levels of greenhouse gas emissions (see Chapter 5). It is also possible that congestion charges in major cities will be introduced and will work well. In the meantime, we in the UK have settled for a politically acceptable level of fuel tax which does not upset farmers or hauliers too much.

Figure 24 shows how fuel taxes compare. Few countries have made significant progress towards meeting internationally agreed limits on greenhouse gas emissions.

The business response

Businesses have not stood by and simply watched the development of environmental pressures. There have been many reasons for them to develop their own policy response.

- Some businesses have identified market niches which created opportunities.

- Businesses have increased spending on research and development, honing their expertise in the design of environmentally friendlier products and processes.

The climate change levy

Introduced in 2001, the climate change levy taxes business use of electricity and fossil fuels. It was designed so that overall it would cost nothing for the business sector as a whole. The idea was that energy users would pay the tax, but the proceeds would all be returned to businesses in the form of lower employers' national insurance contributions. This would create an incentive for all energy users to economize on the amount used.

In practice, the big energy users tend to be mostly manufacturers. Early estimates suggest that the tax will raise input costs by about 1 per cent. In addition to taxing manufacturers of the end product, the levy affects suppliers' costs, so their prices rise too. There is thus an indirect effect as well as a direct one.

Some people deeply dislike the climate change levy. However, Paul Reeve of the Engineering Engineers Federation said: 'There are plenty of opportunities to improve the levy and achieve the environmental gains in a way that does not harm the competitiveness of manufacturing.'

- Some businesses have developed far-reaching environmental policies which have had some effect.

- The use of environmental or energy audits has drawn attention to the scope for action as well as revealing cost savings.

- The enhanced reputation which may result from all the above can be a valuable asset to the business.

It has been claimed by some businesses that a strong culture of environmental responsibility is good business practice and not necessarily detrimental to long-term profitability. However, to make a real difference, environmental policies have to be fully integrated into the strategies adopted by the business. They cannot be mere statements of intent but must be translated into action. This may involve having appropriate training programmes so that all employees understand the nature of the firm's environmental objectives and how best to implement them.

Environmental audits

Some businesses have introduced environmental audits which look at every aspect of their activities and carefully analyse their impact on the environment. This will mean looking at the amount of energy used, any pollution caused, the amount of waste and methods of waste disposal, how much recycling takes place, and so on. If targets have been set for environmental impact, then an audit allows progress towards the target

---

B&Q to go peat-free

The long-term future of some of the UK's finest wildlife sites was given a considerable boost today after it was revealed that B&Q, the leading home and garden chain (with 30 per cent market share), is planning to go completely peat-free. The move follows concerns over the environmental impacts of peat extraction.

The company's plans will send shock waves through the highly competitive home and gardening retail sector, and should lead to a rush of investment into composting facilities for the production of peat-free alternatives.

The UK's lowland raised peatbogs are amongst the most important and valuable wildlife habitats we have. They are home to many important species of birds, a wealth of unusual plants and thousands of rare insect species. Only a fragment of near-natural bog remains in the UK.

Source: Press release from Friends of the Earth, 16 April 2001

---

to be measured.

Sainsbury's have been very active in this respect. They (and B&Q) audit their supplier companies' as well as their own activities. Some businesses audit the environmental impact of some of their products, but not all.

Conclusion

Businesses naturally want to try to compare the costs of environmentally friendly strategies with the likely benefits. If the benefits are clear, some businesses will make progress in making fewer demands on the environment, without further encouragement. If the costs are likely to be high, and the benefits go to society as a whole rather than to the business, then government regulation may be necessary if public opinion requires improvements. Then all businesses face the same problems and their competitive position is not greatly affected.

Difficulties may occur when businesses are competing with producers in countries where environmental regulation is less strict. They will have lower costs. If their governments will not agree, then progress towards sustainable development is slow.

Many of the issues which arise in relation to the environment also figure in the next chapter, on social responsibility.

KEY WORDS

Sustainable development	Negative externalities
Pollution	Pressure groups
Climate change	Hazardous wastes
Congestion	Environmental audits
External costs	

Further reading

Bradburn, R., Chapter 8 in *Understanding Business Ethics*, Continuum, 2001.

Chambers, I., and Gray, D., Unit 35 in *Business Studies*, 2nd edn, Causeway Press, 2000.

Harris, N. (ed.), Chapter 8 in *Change and the Modern Business*, Macmillan, 1997.

Wall, N., 'Taxing fuel: a zero sum game?', *Business Review*, September 2001.

Useful websites

- Friends of the Earth: www.foe.org.

- Unilever: www.unilever.com.

- The Environment Council, an independent charity: www.greenchannel.com/tec.

Essay topic

Using the case of a business which has been the subject of media criticism for its environmental record, explain the criticisms and show how the business tried to improve its reputation. To what extent was it successful?

Data response question

Study the pie chart (Figure A) and Table A, and read the short article. Then answer the questions that follow.

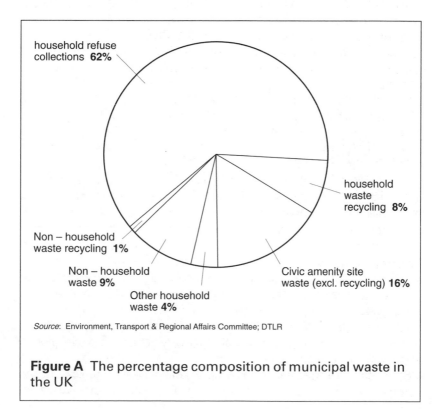

Source: Environment, Transport & Regional Affairs Committee; DTLR

Figure A The percentage composition of municipal waste in the UK

Table A Where the waste goes in England and Wales
(percentages), 1998–99

	Landfill	Incineration	Recycling and composting
Industrial waste	47	6	39
Commercial waste	66	4	29
Municipal waste	83	8	9

Industrial waste excludes construction and demolition waste.

Source: Environment, Transport & Regional Affairs Committee, DTLR.

Dump it or burn it?

You can dispose of waste using a landfill site, an incinerator, by recycling or by composting. From Figure A it is clear that, as far as individuals are concerned, recycling comes a poor second to putting rubbish in the bin or taking it to the local dump. The government's waste strategy says burying rubbish is a waste of valuable resources. It can lead to methane, a greenhouse gas, being released into the atmosphere as the rubbish decomposes.

Does your local council want to build an incinerator close by? If it does, you may have noticed in the local paper that some people have objected. They may even have got their MP to object too. Greenpeace, the pressure group, is campaigning against incinerators, on the grounds that they cause health problems.

The medical journal *The Lancet*, in a report published in 1998, found that women living within 3 km of hazardous-waste landfills had a small but significantly increased risk of having babies with birth defects.

The government is having some difficulty with an EU directive which requires the UK to halve the amount of landfill used for household rubbish between 1995 and 2013. The amount of rubbish we put out is currently growing by 3 per cent a year. The government target for recycling, 30 per cent by 2010, is not ambitious. Austria, Germany and the Netherlands manage 45 per cent *already*.

The landfill tax charged £10 per tonne of waste dumped in 2001 and this charge is planned to rise by a pound every year. This is designed to discourage the use of landfill.

Sunchem Ltd makes paints and a variety of speciality chemicals. It has to dispose of some hazardous wastes as well as normal industrial waste.

1. List the pros and cons of different waste disposal strategies.
   [4 marks]
2. What might be done to comply with the EU directive on landfill?
   [3 marks]
3. How might landfill taxes be likely to affect Sunchem Ltd in the future? [4 marks]
4. How might Sunchem react to higher charges? Evaluate the likely outcome. [5 marks]
5. Are there any potential opportunities for businesses in the present waste disposal situation? Explain your answer. [4 marks]

Chapter Ten

Ethical business

'American managers are too little concerned about their workers.'
Akio Morita, co-founder of Sony

Each of us has an individual set of values which shape our lives and our decisions. In a business there will be people from a wide range of value systems. If the corporate culture of the business makes, say, profit and growth its foremost and only objective, then there is little need for individual values to be discussed among the management team. Few questions arise.

In the past, such a situation was common. The management pursued profit. Employees tried to protect their interests by joining a trade union, with the objectives of improving pay and working conditions. The atmosphere between unions and management would tend often to be confrontational.

Business interest in providing customer service was not often emphasized. Businesses tended to be product-oriented rather than market-oriented in their approach to design and production.

A number of important long run developments made this situation much less tenable.

Intensified competition

Intensified competition put pressure on many businesses. Some of this came from increasing international trade, some from a developing dynamic economy in which there were more business start-ups. Governments steadily strengthened their competition laws too.

All this put pressure on businesses to improve product quality and look for cost savings which would keep prices down. That meant they needed to be able to collaborate effectively with employees, so that they could increase productivity. Collaborating meant making **employee welfare** a much higher priority than it had been.

Customer expectations

Customer expectations rose. Shoddy goods were no longer widely tolerated. To help them compete, many businesses smartened up their customer service approaches, as well as improving quality. Employee training became more important to the success of the business.

Attitudes in society
Attitudes in society changed. In many ways, society became more humane. Discrimination was no longer socially acceptable. Working conditions which involved high accident rates also became unacceptable. Many of the changes were embodied in new laws and regulations.

The business response
The changes described have gradually encouraged businesses to try to base their decisions on what they believe to be ethical, which means morally right. Broadly, they have responded in two ways to the pressure to show more social responsibility.

- Some will make absolutely sure that they comply with the law of the country in which they are operating.

- Others will actually go further than that, devising a **code of practice** which makes their policies clear.

Codes of practice can be used to improve the image of a business. They can also actually change business behaviour. They set out for employees the procedures for dealing with situations in which ethical considerations may be relevant. They may cover environmental issues and corporate integrity – which would involve dealing with suppliers and customers, and **stakeholders** generally, in an honest and fair way.

Of course, there are some businesses in which ethics is seen as a nuisance, nothing to do with practical business operations. It will be thought that ethical decisions raise costs and reduce profit. These businesses will comply with the law on a minimalist basis. Or they may be careless about compliance, or even ignore the law. They may have codes of practice which are more for show than for impact.

Rights and wrongs
This is where the difficulties start. Many businesses do get criticized because their decisions are not seen as being ethical, and **pressure groups** attack them. Some of these businesses feel that they have been attacked unreasonably. The ways in which they seek to defend themselves can be positive and lead to a more ethical stance. They can also be designed mainly for show. Many businesses do change, but often not as far as interested pressure groups would like them to.

Businesses which say they comply with the law in every country in which they operate will often be quite correct in that assertion. The complicating factor is that the law protects consumers, employees and the environment to a very limited degree in some countries. For example, low-income countries typically have very weak employment protection laws. Governments may have a real fear that stronger legislation will discourage employers from hiring people and reduce the number of jobs available.

Responsibility to whom?

An ethical business recognizes several groups to which it is responsible. These are the stakeholders, people or groups affected by the decisions of the business. They include:

- customers
- employees
- suppliers
- the community in which the business operates and its environment
- shareholders.

Customers

Businesses have a responsibility to provide their customers with serviceable products, giving good value for money, and appropriate customer service. Large areas of these obligations are covered by consumer protection law. However, many businesses will try to go further, partly for ethical reasons and partly because they value their reputations.

Product safety has become increasingly important in terms of both the law and the company image. Accidents involving the quality of the product or service can be very expensive because of compensation claims. They are also highly embarrassing. They may have a disastrous effect on reputation and the business may not survive a serious event of this sort.

Some ethical businesses refuse to collude with one another. **Collusion** is illegal, but it does happen quite often. Because it leads to higher prices, it is very detrimental to the interests of customers. Those businesses which genuinely avoid it are showing a high degree of responsibility to the consumer.

Employees

The ethical treatment of employees has so many facets that it is impossible to cover all of the angles. However, there are some areas of overriding importance which can be identified.

The Herald of Free Enterprise

In 1987, the ferry *Herald of Free Enterprise* sailed out of Zeebrugge harbour with its bow doors open. Water poured into the main car deck, destabilizing the ship. It turned over and came to rest on its side on a sandbank. In this disaster 188 people died, the worst shipping accident for a UK vessel since the *Titanic*.

The court investigation found that three employees of Townsend Thoresen, the ferry company, had contributed to the disaster. However, the company as a whole was implicated and the finding was unlawful killing – i.e. a crime. There were various systems which the company could have set up to ensure that it operated safely.

This case had some impact on the way businesses think about organization and the systems and rules which are needed to deal with safety issues.

- *Safety* – Health and safety at work is a most basic factor in the treatment of employees. Many aspects of health and safety are covered by UK law. However, businesses vary as to the care they take in complying.

- *Pay* – Low pay is widespread in some occupations. Obviously it is unethical to pay less than the minimum wage in the country concerned. However, some minimum wage levels are low in relation to the cost of living. Some businesses will look to pay above the average rate for the occupation. They may do this either for ethical reasons or because they believe that there are advantages in terms of employee loyalty, or perhaps some mixture of the two.

- *Trade union activity* – Trade union recognition is not always easy to achieve, although recent changes in the law make better provision for this. Without union recognition, it is very difficult for unions to help their members achieve improved pay and working conditions. Some businesses do manage to discourage union membership quite actively. It can be argued that this is not an ethical position because employee rights are being curtailed.

A number of employers (for example, Boots) are committed to being flexible about family needs. This can involve providing part-time work which fits in with childcare arrangements, or allowing more time off for children than the law requires. Some employers think this gives them a better choice of potential good recruits.

Other employers are happy for a 'long hours culture' to develop. Business experts have begun to point out that working long hours does not always mean that employers are getting the best out of their employees.

Outsourcing and employees

A major problem arises when a business starts outsourcing its inputs. The suppliers from which it buys may or may not adopt an ethical approach to employee relations.

Nike has been heavily criticized for using very poorly paid workers to make its products. In practice, these people are employed in countries such as Indonesia and Vietnam by the businesses from which Nike buys. There is very little employee protection in the countries concerned. For some time, Nike hoped to fend off criticism on the grounds that the people concerned were better off with jobs than without.

Pressure group action has forced Nike to try to improve the pay and conditions of workers in its suppliers' factories. At the time of writing it is hard to tell how successful (or widespread) these efforts have been.

What is absolutely certain is that employees do receive lower pay in developing countries. That is what makes locating production there attractive. Low wages contribute to cuts in the prices which consumers have to pay for the product. Furthermore, many of the employees *are* better off than they would have been without the job.

These issues are controversial, but few governments discourage the growth of exports.

McDonald's

A number of allegations have been made about McDonald's lack of enthusiasm for trade unions on their premises. It appears that they do not like trade unions to attempt to recruit their employees. A spokesperson for USDAW, the shop workers union, said: 'All we want is an opportunity to present our case to the workforce and get them to vote on whether they want union recognition.'

McDonald's has a system of franchises which means that, technically, each outlet is a separate business. This makes it difficult for a trade union to organize McDonald's employees as a group. McDonald's UK denies that it is anti-union and says that most disputes have been in the past and outside the UK.

A company statement on the issue says: 'A diverse team of well-trained individuals working in partnership with the company is the key to success.'

Suppliers

One element in an ethical approach is to ensure that suppliers are treated fairly. Many small suppliers are very dependent on one or a few big customers. They may lack the market power to stand up to them. There have been some complaints about supermarket chains beating down farmers' prices. They can do this because many of their suppliers compete strongly with one another.

In 2000, the UK Competition Commission found 27 ways in which supermarkets were acting against the public interest. These included asking suppliers to pay for visits to their premises by buyers, seeking compensation for unexpectedly low profits, and requiring payment for stocking the suppliers' products.

Some suppliers will be located in developing countries. Pressure groups have drawn attention to the low prices which many third world producers get for their output and to the poor working conditions which are often found. Sainsbury's has made an effort to deal with these issues.

The Fairtrade Foundation gives its approval to products for which a fair price has been paid. Cafedirect is the best known fair trade product. It claims to have helped many farmers to stay in business when world market prices of coffee dropped. Sainsbury's, among others, are stocking Fairtrade products.

The community

Many ethical issues relate to local problems. For example, new property developments may lead to congested roads. Sometimes in the

---

Socially responsible sourcing

'We are working with the suppliers of Sainsbury's own-brand goods to implement our Code of Practice for socially responsible sourcing. Covering issues like health and safety, equal opportunities and the protection of children, the Code aims to make sure that basic employment conditions, based on internationally agreed International Labour Organization standards, are in place.

Aside from our internal activities, Sainsbury's is also a founding member of the Ethical Trading Initiative, an association which brings together retailers, trade unions and international charities like Oxfam and Christian Aid. Its purpose is to agree standards for third world suppliers and methods for monitoring performance.'

Source: Sainsbury's website

UK planning permission for these will be made conditional on the provision of road improvements. Polluting plant has a very obvious effect on the community. Some businesses are particularly concerned to create a good relationship with the people who live around their facilities. BP, the oil company, for example, has an extensive community programme which is partly focused on the area around BP's installations.

For multinationals, the communities in which they operate may be all over the world. Some of the biggest difficulties result from the weak position of local communities in developing countries. Dams have been a particular cause for concern. The contractor may have been able to agree the project with the government of the country concerned. The local communities may be ignored, although some have been supported by pressure groups from near and far.

There are numerous examples of big projects, with serious environmental and social consequences, which have gone ahead despite the disquiet of local people.

Shareholders or stakeholders?

At the heart of the idea of ethical business lies the view that businesses are responsible not only to their shareholders, but also to their customers, employees, suppliers and the community in which they operate. Although social responsibility has become an important objective for many businesses, there are still many people who believe that the job of management is to maximize returns for shareholders.

The role of the shareholder is to provide finance, in return for a share of the profits. Shareholders in successful companies may make money.

The Ilusu dam

Balfour Beatty is planning to build the Ilusu dam in Turkey on the Tigris River, forty miles upstream from the Turkish/Iraqi/Syrian border. It will flood 15 towns and 52 villages and displace 78 000 Kurdish people. Balfour Beatty is seeking a £200 million export credit from the UK government to build the dam, which fails to meet World Commission on Dams standards in numerous respects.

Friends of the Earth bought £30 000 of Balfour Beatty shares and attended the company's Annual General Meeting. They hoped to get other shareholders to support their campaign for higher environmental and social standards.

Postscript, 2002: Balfour Beatty have pulled out of the consortium which is building the dam. It may not now be built.

They will be rewarded for providing finance. However, some successful companies also have a strong culture of social responsibility. Indeed, some would say that responsible business strategies are actually good for profit. The difficulty is that some businesses do make considerable profits from doing the ethical minimum and not being at all careful even to be always legal.

The shareholders sign up for the risks involved. Generally, the riskier the business, the higher the potential returns – but, of course, things can go wrong. The whole point of the market system is to encourage efficiency by letting high-cost, high-price producers go out of business. Inefficient producers are not going to make money for shareholders. It is up to the buyer of shares to avoid businesses with problems that may lead to losses.

Social audits

Some businesses are careful to monitor the social impact of their decisions. They will produce a report or a **social audit** each year which details the progress made towards their stated objectives. These will reflect the firm's declared responsibilities towards a number of stakeholder groups. Some businesses produce an environmental audit, others will incorporate an evaluation of environmental impact in a social audit.

Businesses may carry out a social or environmental audit on their suppliers, just as they do on their own activities. This ensures that all the processes which contribute to the final product are examined for their social impact.

Social audits need to include suitable performance indicators relating

Railtrack

In late 2000, the cumulative impact of several rail crashes brought about a massive review of safety and greatly increased Railtrack's costs. The media resounded with statements such as 'people before profit' and some documented evidence that safety work may have been neglected at times.

By late 2001 Railtrack's situation had deteriorated to the point where receivers were called in to run the company. It had run out of money and the government had refused to pay out any more.

The shareholders had lost money. They bought the shares at the time when the government privatized the railways and prospects looked good. They were extremely vocal in protesting about their likely losses and asking for some compensation from the government.

to non-financial objectives. These can be used to measure progress towards particular goals. They could include health and safety data (for example accident rates), minimum rates of pay, or the level of giving to community projects. Full reporting does inspire public confidence.

Responsible profit

You may recall earlier chapters in which the difficulties of policing business were indicated. Why does the Office of Fair Trading need the power to carry out dawn raids (Chapter 7)? Why do companies have to be prosecuted for allowing leaks of hazardous substances (Chapter 9)? There are many cases in which businesses wear a mask of social responsibility. However, it is likely that the general move to be more responsible has created benefits for all stakeholders, including some shareholders.

In recent years there has been strong growth in ethical investment funds. These funds vary as to the businesses they avoid, but they may undertake not to invest customers' money in the shares of businesses which produce arms or tobacco products, or have poor reputations for their environmental or employment policies. If ethical funds turn out to be profitable, it will be an indication that ethical policies can be good for business.

KEY WORDS

Employee welfare	Product safety
Social responsibility	Collusion
Code of practice	Outsourcing
Stakeholders	Social audit
Pressure groups	

Further reading

Bradburn, R., Chapter 10 in *Understanding Business Ethics*, Continuum, 2001.

Campbell, D., Stonehouse, G., and Houston, B., Chapter 14 in *Business Strategy*, Butterworth–Heinemann, 1999.

Surridge, M., 'Social reporting', *Business Review*, September 2001.

Surridge, M., and Gillespie, A., Chapter 6, 'External Influences, The Social Environment' in *AS Business Studies*, Hodder & Stoughton, 2001.

Useful websites

The following are all good sites to visit:

● www.ibe.org.uk

● www.mcspotlight.org

● www.ethicaltrade.org/

● www.sainsburys.co.uk.

Essay topic

How might a business develop an ethical policy and put it into practice? In your answer, use examples of the different possible elements in an ethical approach to business, drawn from a range of different types of business.

Data response question

Read the short piece below and then answer the questions that follow.

BITC awards

The government is trying to encourage social responsibility. In turn, businesses want government departments to be socially responsible too.

The Department of Trade and Industry (DTI) sponsors annual Business in the Community (BITC) awards. BITC believes that if progress is to be made, businesses must be encouraged to act for good business reasons.

Regulation does tend to impose burdens, especially on small companies. If they believe that social responsibility is actually good business practice, they will adopt appropriate policies on their own initiative.

1. List the ways in which socially responsible business decisions may lead to improved profits.   [3 marks]
2. To what extent are the decisions you have identified likely to increase costs?   [4 marks]
3. Why might the government want to foster social responsibility in business?   [3 marks]
4. Evaluate the impact on business decision-making of two different pressure groups.   [6 marks]
5. What consequences might follow from government departments being more socially responsible?   [4 marks]

Conclusion

The external influences on businesses are many and varied. They add up to a big subject and it is quite hard to cover them adequately in one small book. Furthermore, no two people would necessarily agree completely on what to include.

This book has tried to provide a range of real-world examples which is varied enough to show how the main external influences affect different types of business.

An individual business will be affected by a particular selection of significant external factors. The relevant factors will vary in different types of business. For example, with luxury goods and services, income levels are important in determining market demand. For vegetable growers, they generally are not. The business cycle will have a very different impact on these two types of business.

When decisions must be taken, managers have first to work out which external influences are likely to be important for the decision in question. Then they must decide what changes are likely, and what impact these will have on the business. On any of these levels they may make a mistake with regrettable results.

Similarly, when examination questions call for a business strategy to be developed, it is often necessary to work out what the relevant external influences may be. The question may make absolutely no mention of external influences on the business environment, yet a good answer will require some consideration of the significant factors. The main subject of the question may be investment appraisal, but an impending recession may reduce sales revenue, calling into question the usefulness of the calculations about rates of return. Of course, if the product is a vegetable, comment on possible recession would be irrelevant. Both logic and common sense are needed to fit the answer to the situation in hand.

Some external influences affect many, perhaps most businesses. Changes in employment legislation are a case in point. Other external influences affect some businesses but not others. Environmental regulations have more impact on chemical manufacturers than on retailers. Competition law is more likely to affect two large businesses planning a merger than any smaller business.

Business responses to external influences vary hugely. Analysis of external influences, especially in the context of the individual business, gives an extra dimension to thinking about business strategies. It complicates most situations but also makes them endlessly interesting.

Index

market research 10, 20, 27, 73–4
market segments 67, 69, 71
market share 19–21
markets 3, 27, 67, 71, 98–9
mergers 80, 82
minimum wage 82–3, 117
monetary policy 33, 41–6, 48, 50
Monetary Policy Committee 43–5
monopoly 16–17, 80, 82
multi-skilling 60

national insurance contributions
   96
New Deal 97
new product development 18, 58
niche markets 71, 108
non-price competition 4, 20–1

Office of Fair Trading 22, 78–82
Ofgem 78, 91
oligopoly 16–17
outsourcing 118–9

parental leave 87
patents 17, 58–59
PEST analysis 66
pollution 102–4
population change 67–9
Porter, M., 23
pressure groups 105, 116, 119–20
price competition 18–20
price leader 15
price war 18–19
prices 16–20
privatised industries 78, 91–3
process innovation 9, 56, 59–61
product development 56
product innovation 56–8
productivity 60–2, 91
profit 5–8, 18–19, 31, 42, 55, 114
profit-signalling mechanism 6–8,
   58
public spending 94–5

recession 29–32, 42–3, 45–7
recovery 29, 33
red tape 41
regulation 78, 83, 91–3, 103, 106,
   110
research and development (R & D)
   58, 97, 108
restrictive practices 6, 68–76, 80–1

safety standards 74
Sale of Goods Act 79
single market 82, 91
skilled labour 11–12
skills shortages 33
slump 29–30, 32, 47
social attitudes 66, 71–4
social audits 122
Social Chapter 86, 94
social responsibility 116–22
social structure 66, 69–70
stakeholders 115–6, 121–2
sub cultures 71
suppliers 119–20
supply 5–6, 9

taxes 46–7, 95–6, 106
technological change 29, 55–63
technology 8–9, 19, 55
time lags 32, 35–6, 45
tradable permits 106
trade barriers 98–9
Trade Descriptions Act 68, 79
trade union law 85
trade unions 74–5, 85, 114, 118
transparent pricing 50

unemployment 30, 32–3, 41, 51,
   62–3
unfair competition 22
unfair dismissal 86

values 71, 74, 114–5

World Trade Organisation (WTO)
   36, 99
Working Time Directive 86